WILDFLOWERS

of the PACIFIC NORTHWEST

for kids

WILDFLOWERS of the PACIFIC NORTHWEST for kids

Ashley Erdely

Timber Press
Portland, OR

Timber Press
Workman Publishing
Hachette Book Group, Inc.
1290 Avenue of the Americas
New York, New York 10104
timberpress.com

Timber Press is an imprint of Workman Publishing, a division of Hachette Book Group, Inc. The Timber Press name and logo are registered trademarks of Hachette Book Group, Inc.

Printed in Shenzhen, China (APO) on responsibly sourced paper
Text & cover design by Bologna Sandwich

ISBN 978-1-64326-434-9

A catalog record for this book is available from the Library of Congress.

Today the average American school-child can recognize more than a hundred corporate logos. They can give a name to about ten plants, and these include such categories as “Christmas Tree” and “Grass.” We have lost an entire vocabulary, of speech, of experience, and of relationship.

—Robin Wall Kimmerer

PREFACE

Dearest Reader,

The idea for this book was born on the banks of the John Day River. I sprinted down the beach with four children ages six and under, chasing a captivating butterfly. Using an illustrated field guide, the children easily identified the butterfly we found based on the drawings. They handed over the book and begged me to read all about their butterfly to them. I read the entire page aloud—three vague facts about its scientific name, size, and migration region. At the end of the page, their faces scrunched up in confusion. "What about the butterfly?" they challenged. What does it eat? Where does it live? Why is it called that? Their questions went on and on. I told them, regretfully, that there wasn't any more information in the book, so we'd have to research more (days later) when we got home. Their faces dropped. The field guide that was supposed to teach them about their butterfly had let them down, and the perfect learning moment was over.

I humbly reflected on a recent hiking experience where, despite having my backpack loaded with wildflower field guides, I struggled to remember more than a handful of species at the end of the day—and still, all I had learned about them were their names. At that exact moment, it became clear that a new field guide was needed—one that was engaging, meaningful, and fun. So, with a combination of my experience as a teacher and parent in great collaboration with local botanists and more than one hundred young naturalists, *Wildflowers of the Pacific Northwest for Kids* was born. Although originally inspired by a butterfly, this book features native wildflowers that won't fly away on you, so you can enjoy observing them as long as you'd like.

Happy exploring,

Ashley

Land Acknowledgment and Dedication

With heartfelt gratitude, I would like to take this opportunity to acknowledge and appreciate the Indigenous people of the land we now call the Pacific Northwest. Their wisdom, experiences, and sacrifices must be honored and not forgotten. By including traditional uses for the wildflowers within the pages of this book, I intend to value their wisdom, keep Indigenous histories alive, and work toward honoring and remembering their ways and their truth.

This book is dedicated to the Breeze Sisters and all the young naturalists who explore the Pacific Northwest; may the wildflowers within these pages instill a sense of connection, wonder, and compassion for the natural world around you.

Disclaimers

Never eat any part of a wild plant unless you're 100 percent certain of its identification and how to consume it safely.

The information in this book is true and complete to the best of our knowledge. All recommendations are made without guarantee on the part of the author or Timber Press. The author and publisher disclaim any liability in connection with the use of this information. In particular, eating wild plants is inherently risky. Plants can be mistaken easily, and individuals vary in their physiological reactions to plants that are touched or consumed.

CONTENTS

QUICK REFERENCE

Composite Flowers

Counting the number of blooms on a plant is not always easy because looks can be misleading. Sunflowers and daisies appear to be one large flower surrounded by a ring of long petals, but they are actually what we call composite flowers. Each bloom is made up of dozens upon dozens of miniature flowers called florets.

When a honeybee visits a composite flower, like a sunflower, it's actually visiting hundreds of tiny flowers. Hard to imagine? Check out the diagram on the inside cover of this book, then grab a magnifying glass and a sunflower or turn to the entry about arrowleaf balsamroot on page 86. Look closely at one of the long, yellow "petals" and prepare to be surprised. These petals are not just petals. Each is a tiny, complete ray flower made of one large petal (the long petal you noticed first) and several smaller ones at the base. But don't stop your investigation there: Look at the bumpy surface of the flower inside the ring of ray flowers. These little bumps are also flowers—each is a tiny, five-petaled disk flower. Can you see the tiny petals forming miniature flowers, or florets? Step back and admire how all these tiny florets create the illusion of one much larger flower. You'll likely never look at a sunflower the same way again.

Blooming Wildflowers by Month

	FEBRUARY	MARCH	APRIL	MAY	JUNE	JULY	AUGUST	SEPTEMBER	OCTOBER
Arrowleaf Balsamroot			✿	✿	✿	✿			
Arrow-leaf Buckwheat				✿	✿	✿			
Beargrass				✿	✿	✿	✿		
Bitterroot			✿	✿	✿				
Bleeding Heart			✿	✿	✿				
Bluebell				✿	✿	✿	✿	✿	
Broadleaf Lupine					✿	✿	✿		
Broadleaf Stonecrop			✿	✿	✿				
California Poppy				✿	✿	✿	✿	✿	
Camas			✿	✿	✿				
Chocolate Lily			✿	✿	✿				
Columbia Lily				✿	✿	✿	✿		
Cow Parsnip					✿	✿	✿		
Death Camas			✿	✿	✿				
Desert Parsley			✿	✿	✿				
Early Blue Violet			✿	✿	✿	✿	✿		
Explorer's Gentian						✿	✿	✿	✿
Fireweed				✿	✿	✿	✿	✿	

	FEBRUARY	MARCH	APRIL	MAY	JUNE	JULY	AUGUST	SEPTEMBER	OCTOBER
Fragrant Fringecup			✿	✿	✿	✿			
Glacier-lily		✿	✿	✿	✿	✿	✿		
Gold-star	✿	✿	✿	✿	✿				
Grass Widow	✿	✿							
Great Purple Monkey-flower					✿	✿	✿		
Hooker's Fairy-bell			✿	✿	✿	✿			
Large-flowered Tritelia			✿	✿	✿				
Leafybract Aster						✿	✿	✿	
Long-leaf Phlox			✿	✿	✿				
Miner's Lettuce			✿	✿	✿				
Monkey-flower		✿	✿	✿	✿	✿	✿	✿	
Oregon Sunshine				✿	✿	✿	✿		
Piggyback				✿	✿	✿	✿		
Poet's Shooting Star		✿	✿	✿					
Prairie Star			✿	✿	✿				
Red Columbine				✿	✿	✿			
Rocky Mountain Iris				✿	✿	✿			
Sagebrush Mariposa Lily				✿	✿	✿			

	FEBRUARY	MARCH	APRIL	MAY	JUNE	JULY	AUGUST	SEPTEMBER	OCTOBER
Scarlet Gilia				✿	✿	✿	✿		
Scarlet Paintbrush				✿	✿	✿	✿	✿	
Showy Milkweed					✿	✿	✿		
Shrub Penstemon				✿	✿	✿	✿	✿	
Skunk Cabbage		✿	✿	✿	✿	✿			
Small-flowered Blue-eyed Mary		✿	✿	✿	✿	✿			
Taper-tip Onion				✿	✿	✿			
Trillium		✿	✿	✿	✿				
Twinflower				✿	✿	✿	✿	✿	
Upland Larkspur		✿	✿	✿	✿	✿	✿		
Western Buttercup			✿	✿	✿				
White Bog Orchid					✿	✿	✿	✿	
Yarrow	✿	✿	✿	✿	✿	✿	✿	✿	✿
Yellow Bells		✿	✿	✿	✿				

Blooming Wildflowers by Elevation

	LOW ELEVATION	MIDDLE ELEVATION	HIGH ELEVATION
Arrowleaf Balsamroot	✿	✿	
Arrow-leaf Buckwheat	✿	✿	✿
Beargrass	✿	✿	✿
Bitterroot	✿	✿	
Bleeding Heart	✿	✿	
Bluebell	✿	✿	✿
Broadleaf Lupine		✿	✿
Broadleaf Stonecrop		✿	
California Poppy	✿		
Camas	✿	✿	
Chocolate Lily	✿	✿	✿
Columbia Lily	✿	✿	✿
Cow Parsnip	✿	✿	
Death Camas	✿	✿	
Desert Parsley	✿	✿	
Early Blue Violet	✿	✿	✿
Explorer's Gentian	✿	✿	✿
Fireweed	✿	✿	✿
Fragrant Fringecup	✿	✿	
Glacier-lily	✿	✿	✿

	LOW ELEVATION	MIDDLE ELEVATION	HIGH ELEVATION
Gold-star	✿	✿	
Grass Widow	✿	✿	
Great Purple Monkey-flower		✿	✿
Hooker's Fairy-bell	✿	✿	
Large-flowered Tritelia	✿	✿	
Leafybract Aster	✿	✿	✿
Long-leaf Phlox	✿	✿	
Miner's Lettuce	✿	✿	
Monkey-flower	✿	✿	
Oregon Sunshine	✿	✿	✿
Piggyback	✿	✿	
Poet's Shooting Star	✿		
Prairie Star	✿	✿	
Red Columbine	✿	✿	
Rocky Mountain Iris	✿	✿	✿
Sagebrush Mariposa Lily	✿	✿	
Scarlet Gilia	✿	✿	✿
Scarlet Paintbrush	✿	✿	✿
Showy Milkweed	✿		
Shrub Penstemon	✿	✿	✿

	LOW ELEVATION	MIDDLE ELEVATION	HIGH ELEVATION
Skunk Cabbage	✿	✿	
Small-flowered Blue-eyed Mary	✿	✿	✿
Taper-tip Onion	✿	✿	
Trillium	✿	✿	
Twinflower	✿	✿	✿
Upland Larkspur	✿	✿	✿
Western Buttercup	✿	✿	
White Bog Orchid	✿	✿	✿
Yarrow	✿	✿	✿
Yellow Bells	✿	✿	

WILD ABOUT WILDFLOWERS

The Pacific Northwest: A Wildflower Wonderland

Spring in the Pacific Northwest unfolds like a vivid storybook as birds return from their winter retreats, mud puddles appear, animals give birth to their young, and the muted landscape of winter bursts into a kaleidoscope of colorful, vibrant wildflowers. The Pacific Northwest, from Northern California all the way up to Southern British Columbia, Canada, is a wonderland for more than 1,200 unique and captivating wildflower species.

Why do so many wildflowers grow here?

It all started 2.6 million years ago during the Ice Age, when the Great Continental Ice Sheet advanced and retreated between Canada and the Northern United States roughly tewnty times, drastically changing the land and altering the sea level depth by 300 feet. Then, about 14,000 years ago, powerful floods and glaciers (enormous chunks of ice up to 2.5 miles thick) flowed through what is now known as the Pacific Northwest, carving and eroding the land. About 16,000 square miles of grasslands, plains, and river valleys drastically changed as a result, forming diverse landscapes, including the coastal shores of the Pacific Ocean, deserts, lakes, mountain ranges, rivers, and volcanoes.

You might wonder what all of this has to do with wildflowers. As you explore these different microclimates—small restricted areas different from the climate around them—you can see how diverse each is from the next based on the plants and animals you find there. The weather of each microclimate plays a significant role in influencing which plants and animals live there. For example, areas closer to the Pacific Ocean receive more rain and

THE PACIFIC NORTHWEST
Garibaldi Park
Kamloops
Tsilos Provincial Park
British Columbia
Banff National Park
Vancouver
North Cascades National Park
Olympic National Park
Seattle
Spokane
Leavenworth
Tacoma
Washington
Mt. Rainier National Park
Idaho Panhandle National Forests
Vancouver
Columbia River Gorge
Cannon Beach
Portland
Salem
Wallowa Mountains
Idaho
Coos Bay
Eugene
Oregon
Rogue River-Siskiyou National Forest
Crater Lake National Park
Boise
Medford
Klamath National Forest
Eureka
Northern California

« The Pacific Northwest, from Northern California all the way up to Southern British Columbia, Canada, is a wonderland for more than 1,200 unique and captivating wildflower species.

precipitation than those on the drier side of a mountain range closer to the desert. What wildflowers might you expect to see on your next trip to the desert? How would they compare with those you might see at the coast?

Elevation, or how high you are above sea level, also influences where wildflowers can survive. As you hike up a mountain trail, you may notice that the types of wildflowers blooming change at different elevations. The California poppies and trillium that grow near the low-elevation trailhead are replaced by columbine and lupine the higher you climb. Pay attention to the wildflowers growing around you as you wander in and out of the forest canopy. Which species prefer shade? Which thrive in more direct sunlight? When you finally reach the summit, you'll be greeted by species of alpine wildflowers, such as penstemon and paintbrush, rewarding you with a glorious view from the top.

The Pacific Northwest is built upon many rock types, including basalt, granite, limestone, sandstone, and serpentine. Over time, these different rocks erode to create diverse soil types and depths, also influencing which plants can grow there. Wildflowers need specific growing conditions to survive, and the diversity of the Pacific Northwest provides suitable homes for a wide variety of species. This is why, on a single, short hike, you may pass through many microclimates, each with its unique flower combination that grows well with the specific soil, temperature, sunlight, and other environmental factors in that area.

Once a wildflower finds its ideal place to grow, you can count on that species returning to the same location year after year. The fun part is trying to predict when. Different species bloom at different times, so visiting your favorite wildflower places

California poppies are considered native wildflowers in most of the Pacific Northwest, except Washington state, where they are considered invasive weeds. »

regularly throughout the seasons is important to discovering which wildflowers have emerged and which are yet to bloom.

Pay attention to these floral wonders, each beckoning you to uncover the stories woven into their petals. Aside from being beautiful, wildflowers serve essential roles for animals, humans, and our environment. Wildflowers provide pollen and nectar for pollinators as well as food and shelter for other animals and insects. Humans have used wildflowers for centuries to make medicines, natural dyes and paints, perfumes, toys, food, tea, and more. What wildflowers do you use in your daily life? How might your world be different without wildflowers?

Wildflower or Weed?

Wildflower: (noun) *A naturally occurring, seed-producing flower that grows without the help of humans*

Weed: (noun) *A naturally occurring, seed-producing flower that grows without the help of humans in a place where it's not wanted*

By their definitions, wildflowers and weeds are exactly the same, except for one difference: Weeds, stemming from the Old English word *weod*, meaning unwanted or small, are considered annoying and unwelcome. This means that the decision to label a flowering plant growing naturally as either a beautiful wildflower or a pesky weed all comes down to our perspective.

Is the glass half full or half empty? Is a dandelion a wildflower or a weed? A young child might delight in seeing a field of dandelions ready for braiding into flower crowns or blowing wishes

upon. A gardener, however, who finds a dandelion growing uninvited in their tidy yard, may have a different view and see it as a problematic weed that needs to be removed. An herbalist may see a dandelion as an essential herb for making a healing tea or salve. And a chef may see it as a ripe ingredient for spicing up a seasonal salad or making tasty vinegar. In the words of Susan Wittig Albert, "One person's weed is another person's wildflower." It all depends on our perspective.

Native, Endangered, Invasive—Oh, My!

Wildflowers fall into different classification categories based on the habitat in which they grow. Some wildflowers are considered native to an area, meaning they have always grown there naturally. It's important to keep in mind that a plant can be considered a helpful native species in one location but a problem in another. When a wildflower is introduced into a place it has never grown before, it's considered an invasive species and a

Columbia parsley is one of 15 endemic species of wildflowers found only in the Columbia River Gorge.

threatening competitor to native plants. This is the case for California poppies, which are considered native in most Pacific Northwest states yet invasive in Washington. Some native plants grow only in one place and are called endemic. The Columbia River Gorge of southern Washington and northern Oregon is home to about fifteen endemic wildflowers, meaning this is the only place in the world you will find them growing naturally.

Wildflowers require specific habitats to thrive. When human or natural causes negatively affect those habitats, the species living there are placed in danger. When a species is at the point that it faces a threat of disappearing permanently, we call it an endangered species. Those species that scientists consider likely to become endangered soon are called threatened species. Thankfully, US programs such as the Endangered Species Act of 1973 help protect and preserve these species. Throughout this book, you will learn ways to help too.

Campanula rotundifolia

Why So Many Names?

Like all living plants and animals, wildflowers have more than one name. You may call the beautiful blue bell-shaped flower growing in your backyard a bluebell, but your friend might call it a harebell. And guess what? You're *both* correct. Bluebell and harebell are examples of common names—names given to wildflowers by everyday people, often chosen to honor Indigenous Americans, famous botanists (scientists who study plants), important places, or to refer to stories of explorers or legends. These common names are often memorable and fun to learn, yet you can imagine how using many different names for one flower might get confusing.

Thankfully, science prioritizes organization. Scientists worldwide have organized a taxonomic system for naming, defining, and classifying all living things. This system ensures that each living plant or animal has its own unique species name. Botanists refer to a wildflower by its scientific name. For example, the scientific name for a bluebell is *Campanula rotundifolia*. The first part of its name, *Campanula*, is its genus name (a group of species scientists consider very closely related), which means "little bell" in Latin. There are many wildflowers with a similar bell shape whose names begin with *Campanula*, so scientists also include the second word in its name, the species name, which serves as an adjective describing its genus name. In the case of *Campanula rotundifolia*, the species name *rotundifolia* means "round leaves," describing these little bells more specifically to ensure proper identification.

Scientific names have fascinating roots and make it possible for botanists worldwide to work together regardless of their location or native language. Scientific or botanical names are always written in Latin.

Wildflowers in Our Changing World

Did you know climate change affects wildflowers? Imagine having a birthday party, but your friends showed up on the wrong day—that's what's happening to wildflowers. Usually, wildflowers bloom on a schedule: they know when to display their colorful petals to attract bees and butterflies. However, climate change is causing the weather to behave unusually. Temperatures are getting warmer and rainfall is unpredictable, resulting in some seasons with too much rain and others with not enough. This confuses the wildflowers, causing them to bloom earlier or later than usual.

With this knowledge in mind, please note that the bloom times written in this book will adjust seasonally along with

Bloom times may vary from year to year.

Wildflowers blooming after a recent wildfire.

Pollinators rely on wildflowers for their survival. »

climate change. For those of us who enjoy wildflower season, this unpredictability keeps us on our toes. However, for the bees and butterflies that depend on wildflowers for food and shelter, this poses a serious problem. Not knowing when or whether the wildflowers they rely upon will bloom puts them at risk for survival.

Like all species, wildflowers adapt over time, adjusting to their changing environments. As our planet warms, some plants won't have the growing conditions they need and, as a result, they won't survive. In recent years, drought-resistant plants—those plants naturally adapted to survive dry growing conditions—have stood out among the survivors. These plants have cells that can get dehydrated without experiencing permanent damage. Many have special water-sucking abilities and thick waxy coatings on their leaves that help retain moisture. Others have tiny hairs that reduce evaporation from the leaf's surface and reflect sunlight away from the leaf to create a cooling effect. These plants also have special abilities to store water in their tissues and control how much water vapor is lost. In addition to drought-resistant plants, those considered fire-resistant—those that do not burn easily—will also do better during the hot, fiery summers that many areas, including the Pacific Northwest, are becoming more accustomed to.

These changes, even the seemingly small ones, affect our environment greatly. As we all work to care for our planet, we must also look out for the wildflowers and the many creatures that rely on them.

HOW TO USE THIS BOOK

Every time she learns the name of a plant, she feels as if she is meeting someone new. Giving a name to something is a way of knowing it.
—Richard Louv, *Last Child in the Woods*

Exploring the more than 1,200 wildflowers found in the Pacific Northwest can feel overwhelming, so I worked closely with local botanists to choose fifty of the most common species in the region, those you're most likely to encounter in your daily lives. Regular sightings and interactions with these wildflowers in your favorite outdoor places create a deep and caring connection to our local natural environment and the species living there. Science tells us that when we connect with nature, a relationship forms, and with it comes the opportunity to care about nature and take responsibility for protecting it.

This book does not need to be read in any particular order. It is designed to be explored in the moment. If you have a question, turn to the quick reference section at the front of the book, or the glossary at the end of the book where you can look up unfamiliar words and extend your learning.

As you explore these pages, you'll see that each wildflower has its own entry. The wildflower entries are grouped by color. Within each color, the flowers are organized by perceived number of petals and height—in that order.

Petal Color

Since the first thing most people notice about a wildflower is its color, the wildflowers in this book are grouped into chapters based on their *main color*. For example, if you find a purple wildflower, turn to the purple section of the book. If a flower has more than one color, focus on the most dominant color.

Perceived Number of Petals

Once you find the correct color section, you will find all the wild-flowers in that section are ordered according to how many petals they have—from fewest to greatest. Be warned—counting petals is not always as easy as it sounds. Whereas most wildflowers have three, four, five, or six petals, some don't have any at all! Sometimes petals are green, so they get mistaken for leaves or other plant parts. To further complicate things, many wildflowers have hundreds of petals and are classified as composite flowers, which you can learn more about in the Quick Reference section of this book.

Plant Height

Once you identify how many perceived petals are present on a wildflower, it's time to pay attention to another key detail—the plant's height. For this reason, within each color, wildflowers with similar numbers of petals are ordered based on their height—from shortest to tallest. Paying attention to height is important because sometimes species in the same family look a lot alike, such as gold-stars, Oregon sunshine, and arrowleaf balsamroot. Their colors and petals are similar in appearance, so knowing how tall a flower will grow might be the clue that helps you identify it correctly.

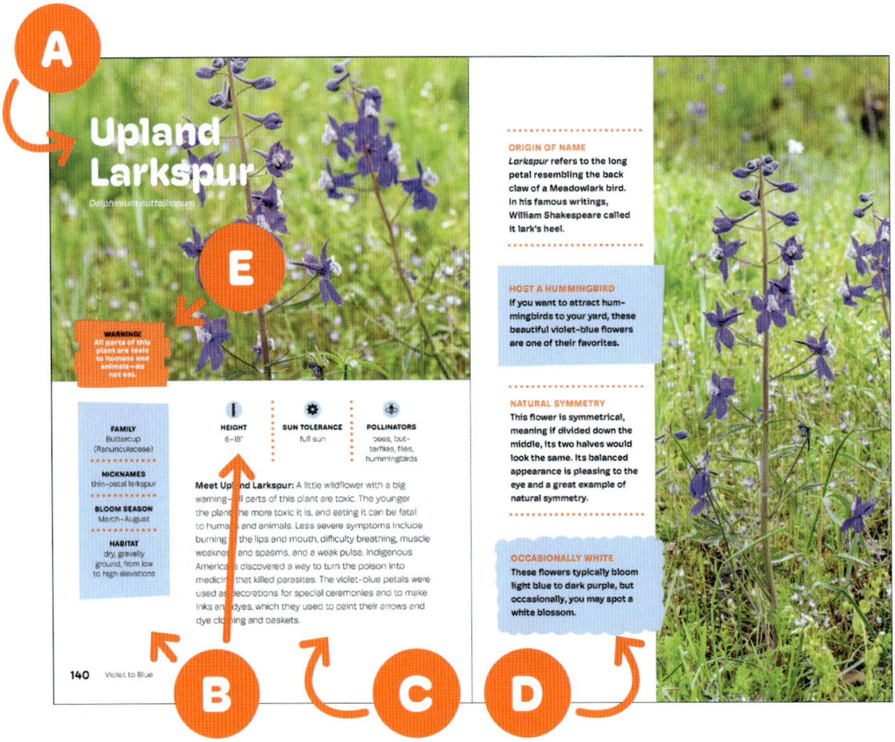

Entry Layout

A Names

Once you locate your wildflower, you will see that each entry displays the wildflower's scientific (botanical) name and common name. Most wildflowers have additional common names, which are listed in this book as nicknames. You will also find quick background information about the origin of each wildflower's name. From Latin roots to ancient legends, each species has its own reason for its unique name.

B Details and Statistics

Other details, such as bloom season, habitat (where they grow), and size, also help us identify a wildflower. Explore the entries further, and you'll find statistics and icons that provide more in-depth knowledge about each wildflower. Since many wildflowers look similar, these statistics will help you correctly identify the wildflowers you find. Furthermore, the same wildflower can have slight differences when growing in different locations, making it tricky to figure out if it's the same species or a similar-looking one. Pay close attention to these statistics.

The more we know about a wildflower, the easier it is to identify it correctly and confidently.

C D Fun Facts and Stories

For many generations, knowledge has been passed on through storytelling. This book is written to feel as though you're reading a story about each wildflower's unique natural and cultural history. These fun facts and stories make the wildflowers interesting and memorable. For example, you may forget that a lupine is also called a sundial, unless you know the story behind the nickname: Lupine petals act like a sundial, tracing the sun's path across the sky throughout the day. And I bet you'll never forget what miner's lettuce is called after you learn that miners ate this leafy wildflower as lettuce during the California gold rush. From the delicate satin petals of a grass widow to the cheerful yellow face of a monkey-flower, each bloom has a unique story to share.

E Warnings

Being safe is always the most important thing. This book uses safety warnings to indicate which wildflowers you should watch out for. Some wildflowers are toxic for humans to eat, and others are poisonous to animals. Furthermore, some wildflowers can be dangerous to touch and cause painful burning sensations or irritating skin rashes. You have probably heard the popular rhyme, leaves of three, let them be, which helps hikers identify poison oak and poison ivy. Some plants have other warning signs, too, like spikes or thorns, that make their danger seen easily, but others do not. The warnings in this book are designed to help you stay safe and have fun. And remember, the best way to avoid pain, illness, or even death from any plant you find in the wild is quite simple: *Do not touch it and do not eat it.*

Some plants provide clues that they are unsafe to touch. Poison oak has leaves that grow in shiny sets of three. It's good to remember, *when you see leaves of three, let them be.*

HOW TO MEET A WILDFLOWER

Here are some simple tips for identifying the wildflowers you find:

Step 1. Find each wildflower in this book by looking at its *petal color, perceived number of petals, and height.*
Study each wildflower carefully. How many colors does it have? What is its main color? Can you count the number of petals easily, or do the petals and leaves look alike? Is the wildflower growing close to the ground or towering in the air? The more you observe about a flower, the easier it will be to identify it.

Step 2. *Leaves* leave clues too.
Leaves offer important clues about a plant and are usually more obvious than petals. Pay attention to the leaves' shape, size, and color. Then, explore deeper. Are the edges smooth, or do they have teeth? Are both sides of the leaf the same color? What is their texture? Are they hairy? Notice where the leaves grow on the plant. Do they grow opposite each other on the stem or climb in alternating steps?

Leaves can also provide important warning signs. Do they look safe to touch? Or, are they covered in sharp, tiny spikes? Some dangerous plants, like poison oak or ivy, have leaves that grow in groups of three. Stay safe with this age-old rhyme: *Leaves of three, let them be.*

Step 3. *Time and place* offer important clues too.
Season, time of day, elevation, and location help us identify wildflowers. When you find a wildflower you want to identify, ask yourself some important questions: What time of year is it?

Because most wildflowers are tiny and grow low to the ground, kids are usually the best at finding them.

Early spring? Late summer? Was the flower blooming in daytime (diurnal) or at night (nocturnal)? Where was it growing? In a forest or a field? By a sandy shore or on a rocky mountain slope? Pay close attention to the statistics about bloom season, habitat, and elevation in each wildflower entry to help you identify the wildflowers you find. And look at the charts in the Quick Reference section for extra help if you need it.

Packing for Success

One of the most essential tips for exploring wildflowers is to think about what you bring along on your hike. Being prepared ensures you stay comfortable and safe. Grab your backpack, follow these packing suggestions, and happy exploring.

- **Comfortable, sturdy, closed-toe shoes** will keep your feet safe and happy.
- Wear **clothing suitable for the weather** and being **outdoors**. Weather changes quickly in the Pacific Northwest, so pack layers.

What is one thing you like to bring with you on a hike?

- Bring **adequate food** and **water** for the length and level of adventure you plan.
- Bring a **map** and **compass** to keep you on the right track. Not only do they sharpen your navigational skills, but they also provide a reliable backup in remote areas with poor cell-phone signals.
- Bring along a lightweight **journal** or **sketchbook** and **some pencils** or **pens**. Unlike birds and other wild animals, wildflowers won't fly or run away from you, so you can sit and sketch for a while.
- Pack a sturdy **magnifying glass** or **hand lens** for up-close investigation.
- Taking a picture with a **camera** or **cell phone** is a great way to remember what a wildflower looks like without picking it. A photo of a wildflower is better for the natural environment, plus it won't wilt in the car on your drive home.
- A small, portable **first-aid kit** is easy to toss in your backpack. If you need a bandage, you'll be glad you did.
- And don't forget to bring along this **field guide**.

Not all of the items listed are required for every occasion and location. Viewing wildflowers doesn't have to happen on a hike. In fact, many wildflowers bloom in parking lots, backyards, playgrounds, and urban areas. All you really need is curiosity. Choose which items are most appropriate and helpful for your adventure.

MEET
WILDFL

THE
OWERS

WHITE

White bog orchids stand tall amidst other wildflowers with a similar bloom season.

Trillium

Trillium ovatum

FAMILY
Lily (Liliaceae)

NICKNAMES
birthroot, toadshade, wake robin

BLOOM SEASON
March–June

HABITAT
open to dense, moist forests, often where boggy in spring, from low to middle elevations

HEIGHT	SUN TOLERANCE	POLLINATORS
6–16"	part shade, full shade	bees, beetles, flies, moths

Meet Trillium: A trillium plant can live up to 25 years and has many uses. Indigenous Americans chewed the root for strength and protection before battle and used the roots to relieve pain during childbirth. Legend also tells of a young girl who wanted the chief's son to fall in love with her, so she boiled trillium roots to make a love potion. While pouring the potion into the young man's food, she tripped. The potion landed in an old man's food instead who, once he finished eating, followed the girl everywhere, begging her to marry him.

ORIGIN OF NAME

Trillium comes from *tri* (three), referring to its triple leaves and petals. *Ovatum* comes from *ovate*, meaning "egg-shaped," and refers to the flower's rounded petal shape.

CHANGING WITH AGE

Trilliums typically bloom white—but don't be fooled if you see one blooming pink or reddish purple. As the white blossom ages, the wavy-edged petals turn pink.

NUMEROUS NAMES

Named wake robin because it was thought to awaken robins in spring, trillium was known as birthroot by Indigenous Americans who recognized its ability to ease pain during childbirth. Its large, umbrella-shaped leaves also earned it the nickname toadshade.

ANIMAL AID

Trillium benefits from a symbiotic relationship with ants and mice. These animals eat the protein-rich fleshy cover of trillium seeds, then carry them back to their nests, unknowingly aiding in seed dispersal and plant reproduction.

Miner's Lettuce

Claytonia perfoliata

FAMILY
Miner's Lettuce (Montiaceae)

NICKNAMES
wild hyacinth

BLOOM SEASON
April–June

HABITAT
open to shady forests, meadows that are seasonally wet, and thickets, from low to middle elevations

HEIGHT
2–12"

SUN TOLERANCE
part shade, full shade

POLLINATORS
flies, self-pollinates

Meet Miner's Lettuce: This wildflower is one of the most well-recognized wild edibles. All parts of the plant are edible—flowers, stems, and roots. Young, tender leaves and stems are typically eaten raw and have a mild flavor similar to spinach. You can also eat the spicy flowers and simmer the roots, although the roots are said to not be as tasty as the greens. Miner's lettuce is edible, but never eat any part of a wild plant unless you're 100 percent certain of its identification and how to consume it safely.

ORIGIN OF NAME

In Latin, *perfoliata* means "to perforate, or pierce a hole." Under the white flower are several leaves fused together, giving the illusion of a single disk-shaped leaf with a hole in the center.

LETTUCE FOR MINERS

In 1848, gold was found in California, which attracted nearly 300,000 gold miners to the area. Miner's lettuce gets its name due to the fact that miners ate the plant as lettuce.

WATCH YOUR SPIT

For fun, chew on miner's lettuce leaves, then spit them out. Did the glowing green color of your saliva surprise you?

NATURE'S VITAMINS

Rich in vitamin C, this wild-flower was a crucial part of the gold miners' diets. They ate it along with chickweed to prevent scurvy, an illness caused by a lack of vitamin C.

White Bog Orchid

Platanthera dilatata

FAMILY
Orchid (Orchidaceae)

NICKNAMES
bog candle, scent bottle, white rein orchid

BLOOM SEASON
June–September

HABITAT
forest openings, streambanks, and wet meadows, from low to high elevations

HEIGHT
12–45"

SUN TOLERANCE
full sun, part shade

POLLINATORS
flies, moths, self-pollination

Meet White Bog Orchid: Scientists estimate there are about 35,000 orchid species—each looking very different from the next, but all brightly colored with slipper-shaped flowers. Nicknamed scent bottle, this wildflower's spicy, clove-like smell attracts pollinators such as flies and moths. Moths prefer this orchid because, being nocturnal, they can see the bright white color easily at night when they are active. White bog orchids can self-pollinate, meaning move pollen from the flower's male part to its female part without the help of pollinators. This is impressive, considering 90 percent of flowering plants cannot self-pollinate and need a pollinator's assistance.

WARNING!
Leaves are toxic—do not eat.

ORIGIN OF NAME

The genus *Platanthera* is Greek and means "broad or wide anther"; *dilatata* means "expanded." Both refer to the enlarged shape of the orchid's petals.

LOOK CLOSELY

Even though they appear to have more, orchids have only three petals. They also have three sepals, the parts of the flower that look like petals but are designed to protect its buds and support its bloom.

USING GRAVITY

These moisture-loving flowers often grow at the bottom of steep slopes, benefiting from runoff water from higher ground above.

LUCK AND LOVE

The Thompson Tribe made a good-luck wash from these flowers: Hunters rinsed their weapons with it before hunting; women used it as a love potion; and men bathed with it hoping to become handsome and sweet-smelling.

Death Camas

Toxicoscordion venenosum

WARNING! This plant is highly poisonous to humans and animals—do not eat.

FAMILY
Lily (Liliaceae)

NICKNAMES
grassy death camas, meadow death camas

BLOOM SEASON
April–June

HABITAT
balds, grasslands, ponderosa pine forest openings, and prairies, from the coast to middle elevations

HEIGHT
12–30"

SUN TOLERANCE
full sun

POLLINATORS
bees

Meet Death Camas: Eating even a very small amount of death camas can be fatal or cause severe reactions including vomiting, lowered body temperature, and difficulty breathing. When not in bloom, its grasslike leaves and underground onion-like bulbs are nearly impossible to differentiate from their edible relative, common camas, which was an essential food source for Indigenous Americans, who had to be extremely careful to harvest the correct bulbs. When the two species are in bloom, it's easy to distinguish the creamy white death camas from the edible purple-blue common camas.

ORIGIN OF NAME

Venenosum comes from the Latin word *venenum*, which means "poison." Does this word remind you of any other words in your language?

SCENT SIGNALS

If you know this flower's name, you will realize its dangers quickly. But for those who don't know its name, the death camas emits a foul smell that deters anyone from getting too close.

POLLINATORS, BEWARE

Miner bees are the only pollinators able to tolerate death camas. The attractive blooms lure other pollinators to try, but most cannot survive the poisonous pollen and nectar, become trapped, and, ultimately, die.

POISON AND PROTECTION

Toxicoscordion is Greek for poison garlic. Indigenous Americans called this wildflower poison onion and often placed it around the perimeter of their homes as protection from evil spirits.

Large-flowered Tritelia

Triteleia grandiflora

WARNING! This plant is poisonous—do not eat.

FAMILY
Lily (Liliaceae)

NICKNAMES
bicolored cluster lily, blue-lily

BLOOM SEASON
April–June

HABITAT
arid prairies, bluffs, and grassy, open slopes, from low to middle elevations

HEIGHT
12–24"

SUN TOLERANCE
full sun, part shade

POLLINATORS
bees, beetles, flies

Meet Large-flowered Tritelia: This wildflower is considered both edible and poisonous at the same time. The Colville-Okanagan people used this plant to make poison. They also ate the underground bulbs (corms) for food. Using a wooden digging stick, they cautiously gathered the nutty-flavored bulbs and boiled or cooked them using an earthen oven. These nutrient-rich bulbs are also an important food source for burrowing rodents like gophers. Large-flowered tritelia is an excellent lesson in why you should never eat any part of a wild plant unless you're 100 percent certain of its identification and how to consume it safely.

ORIGIN OF NAME

Triteleia means "triplet lily" and *grandiflora* refers to its large, or grand, flowers.

WINTER DECORATIONS

These vase-shaped flowers can be dried and used as winter decorations. In Chinese culture, dried lilies represent wealth in the Lunar New Year.

COLORS AS CLUES

Petals are white to light blue, often with deeper blue midline stripes. The stripe's blue shade varies based on where the flower grows: close to the ocean, a deeper blue stripe; farther inland a much lighter blue, even white, stripe.

BARE BLOOMER

This flower has one or two grass-like leaves that wilt and wither away before bloom, leaving tight clusters of flowers alone on a bare stem.

Hooker's Fairy-bell

Prosartes hookeri

WARNING!
The berries of this plant are toxic—do not eat.

FAMILY
Lily (Liliaceae)

NICKNAMES
drops of gold

BLOOM SEASON
April–July

HABITAT
moist, shaded, woody areas, from low to middle elevations

HEIGHT	SUN TOLERANCE	POLLINATORS
12–36"	full shade	bees

Meet Hooker's Fairy-bell: Although Hooker's fairy-bell berries are food for some animals, they are poisonous to humans. Records indicate that a few Indigenous American tribes in inland British Columbia consumed the fruit occasionally, but it wasn't a large part of their diet. Instead, they often used Hooker's fairy-bells for medicine. The Costanoan people used the fruit to create medicine for treating kidneys, while the Makah Tribe used the plant to make a love potion. Never eat any part of a wild plant unless you're 100 percent certain of its identification and how to consume it safely.

ORIGIN OF NAME

The Greek word *prosartes* means "to fasten," which describes how the berries attach securely to this plant. *Hookeri* honors former director of the Royal Botanical Gardens in Kew, England, Sir Joseph Dalton Hooker, who was Charles Darwin's closest friend.

DRIP TIPS

The leaves' shape helps protect the delicate cream-colored flowers during heavy rains. Rainwater runs easily down the slippery parallel-veined leaves and drips off the sharp, pointed leaf tips, forcing the water away from the fragile blooms.

TAKE SHELTER

Up to 6 inches long, the oval leaves also provide shelter from the rain for insects and other small ground-dwelling animals.

BERRIES FOLLOW BLOOMS

Just after bloom, yellow, slightly hairy, egg-shaped berries appear. When the berries mature into a red color, they become a food source for ground-feeding birds like robins and towhees and mammals like chipmunks, squirrels, and wolves.

Beargrass

Xerophyllum tenax

FAMILY
Bunchberry (Melanthiaceae)

NICKNAMES
basket grass, western turkeybeard

BLOOM SEASON
May–August

HABITAT
open woods and clearings, from low to high elevations

HEIGHT
12–60"

SUN TOLERANCE
full sun to full shade

POLLINATORS
bees, beetles, butterflies, flies

Meet Beargrass: Beargrass is important to grizzly bears. They line their dens with its leaves before hibernation. In spring, they hungrily feast on its young stems. Indigenous Americans dyed beargrass leaves and wove them into baskets, capes, and hats and used the roots to make bandages. Beargrass is difficult to grow and can take years to bloom. In recent years, its habitat has decreased because of logging practices, floral industry overharvesting, and other human behaviors. If you spot beargrass, snap a photo or draw a sketch, but please don't pick it—how would grizzlies *bear* living without it?

ORIGIN OF NAME

This plant's scientific name comes from the Greek words *xero*, meaning "dry," and *phyllon*, meaning "leaf," and the Latin word *tenax*, which means "tough." Examine a beargrass leaf. Do you agree with these descriptions?

NAMES AND MISNOMERS

Despite its name and grass-like appearance, this plant is not grass.

BENEATH THE FLUFF

Each plant resembles a giant cotton swab, topped with a big, fluffy, white tuft. Look closely—each tuft is a giant cluster of small, delicate six-petaled flowers.

WILDFLOWERS AND WILDFIRES

Beargrass is fire-resistant and often one of the first species to regrow after a wildfire. However, its habitat decreases as more land is cleared for fire safety.

Cow-parsnip

Heracleum maximum

WARNING! This plant is toxic—do not eat. Contact with the sap can cause skin rashes and blistering.

FAMILY
Umbel/Parsley (Apiaceae)

NICKNAMES
American hogweed

BLOOM SEASON
June–August

HABITAT
moist areas and deep, well-drained soil, from low to middle elevations

HEIGHT
36–120"

SUN TOLERANCE
full sun, part shade

POLLINATORS
bees, bumblebees, flies

Meet Cow-parsnip: In British Columbia, the Carrier people harvested cow-parsnip blossoms to make a bug repellant, which they rubbed on their bodies to keep away flies and mosquitoes. The large leaves were useful for making medicines to treat colds, sore throats, and minor cuts. The most versatile part of this plant, however, is the stem. These large, sturdy stems are hollow and were used commonly as drinking straws for soups and broths. The stems were also tied together to make toy blowguns and homemade flutes. The Cheyenne People performed romantic music on their flutes hoping to impress their sweethearts.

ORIGIN OF NAME

Cow-parsnip is easy to remember because *cows* eat it, and it's in the same plant family as *parsnips*—carrots and parsley too.

NATURE'S HERCULES

Towering 10 feet tall with leaves measuring up to 16 inches across, this giant plant is named *Heracleum*, inspired by Zeus's son Hercules (Herakles in Greek mythology), known for his exceptional strength and size.

LITTLE UMBRELLAS

Each umbrella-like flower cluster is called an umbel. Each umbel is made up of 15 to 30 smaller clusters that can grow up to 8 inches wide.

PASS ON THE PARSNIP

Cow-parsnip is closely related to carrot, celery, and parsley, but please do not eat it. Cows may enjoy it, but it is toxic to humans.

Fragrant Fringecup

Tellima grandiflora

FAMILY
Saxifrage (Saxifragaceae)

NICKNAMES
bigflower tellima

BLOOM SEASON
April–July

HABITAT
damp woods, forest edges, and along streams, from low to middle elevations

HEIGHT	SUN TOLERANCE	POLLINATORS
15–34"	part shade, full shade	birds, hummingbirds, insects

Meet Fringecup: Fragrant fringecup is a favored wildflower for pollinator gardens for its long bloom time. It's also tough against wildfires, making it great for fire-prone areas like the Pacific Northwest. Fringecup also has a rich history of practical and cultural importance to Indigenous American communities. The Upper Skagit people pounded and boiled it to make a healing tea they believed would treat various illnesses and boost appetite. The Ditidaht people referred to it as "special medicine" and used it to ward off nightmares, believing this sweet-smelling flower would, instead, bring sweet dreams.

ORIGIN OF NAME

Fringecup gets its name from its jagged (or deeply fringed) petals surrounding its cup-shaped flowers.

NIGHT VISION

Legend tells us, long ago, forest elves ate fringecup to see better in the dark. Want to improve *your* night vision? Doctors suggest eating more orange-colored fruits and vegetables, which are high in vitamin A.

EMPHASIS ON FRAGRANT

Birds, hummingbirds, and insects are attracted to the strong scent of this wildflower. Conveniently, slugs are not, which makes fringecup a great choice for pollinator gardens.

LEAFING CLUES

Fringecup's fuzzy heart-shaped leaves are evergreen during mild Pacific Northwest winters, making it easy to identify all year.

Yarrow

Achillea millefolium

FAMILY
Composite/Aster (Asteraceae)

NICKNAMES
milfoil, soldier's woundwort

BLOOM SEASON
February–October

HABITAT
open areas, dry to somewhat moist, from low to high elevations

HEIGHT
12–24"

SUN TOLERANCE
full sun, part shade

POLLINATORS
bees, beetles, flies, wasps

Meet Yarrow: Indigenous Americans used yarrow in more than 360 ways. The Navajo called it Sacred Life Medicine, using it to treat many ailments including burns, headaches, respiratory infections, and toothaches—and it is still one of the most popular medicinal herbs. Other tribes made yarrow shampoo and eyewash for their horses. Fragrant seeds were burned as incense in homes and during special ceremonies. Yarrow was and still is used to create various shades of natural yellow and green dyes. Chefs cook with its aromatic leaves to add a bitter, peppery flavor to foods.

ORIGIN OF NAME

Achillea comes from the Greek god Achilles, a hero of the Trojan War who is said to have used this flower to stop his soldiers' bleeding wounds.

SOLDIERS' WOUNDWORT

Yarrow's history as a wound treatment dates back to ancient Greece and continued through the Civil War. Today, it's still a popular medicinal herb for first-aid treatment of minor wounds and nosebleeds.

LITTLE FEATHER

In Spanish, this flower's leaf shape and texture earn it the name *plumajillo* (*ploo-ma-he-o*), meaning "little feather."

NESTING TIME

Soft, sweet-smelling yarrow is used by several cavity-nesting birds, such as Common Starlings, to line their nests.

YELLOW

Wildflowers and rainbows are plentiful during spring months in the Columbia River Gorge.

Skunk Cabbage

Lysichiton americanus

FAMILY
Arum (Araceae)

NICKNAMES
western skunk cabbage

BLOOM SEASON
March–July

HABITAT
bogs, marshes, swamps, and other wetlands, from low to middle elevations

HEIGHT
12–36"

SUN TOLERANCE
full sun, part shade

POLLINATORS
beetles, flies

Meet Skunk Cabbage: Skunk cabbage is considered poisonous, but Indigenous Americans cooked the blossoms during times of near-starvation. This plant had other uses too. Kitasoo children attached the yellow spathes to sticks for throwing contests. The Nuxalk Nation made plant medicine to treat stomach troubles. The Gitksan inhaled the smoke from the roots to treat the flu and bad dreams. Many tribes folded the large leaves and used them as containers, drinking cups, and wraps for cooking bulbs, meat, and roots. Leaves were also woven into mats and used for drying berries.

ORIGIN OF NAME

This flower's common name comes from its skunky smell. Carrion flies, attracted to strong odors, confuse the smell for rotting flesh and commonly lay eggs on it.

BEAR BELLIES

In spring, hungry black bears emerge from hibernation and eat skunk cabbage roots to cleanse and strengthen their stomachs.

SCAVENGING BY SCENT

Scavenging beetles and flies are attracted to skunk cabbage's pungent odor, making them the top pollinators of this plant.

COUNT AGAIN

This native flower has no petals. Instead, it bears four leaf-like sepals, a part of the outer flower surrounding the petals, usually small and green.

Yellow Bells

Fritillaria pudica

FAMILY
Lily (Liliaceae)

NICKNAMES
yellow fritillary

BLOOM SEASON
March–June

HABITAT
shrub-steppe to mixed conifer forests, from low to middle elevations

HEIGHT
4–10"

SUN TOLERANCE
full sun, part shade

POLLINATORS
bees, flies, wasps

Meet Yellow Bells: Indigenous Americans highly valued yellow bells. They dug up the small, underground bulbs for food, eating them fresh, cooked, or dried during winter. Once a common traditional food, yellow bells are eaten only occasionally today. Yellow bells grow in many ecosystems, including the endangered sagebrush steppe. Harvesting bulbs must be done with great care to avoid damaging the surrounding area. Many people believe that yellow bells should be considered a protected species in the sagebrush steppe to protect this fragile environment. Bears, gophers, ground squirrels, and other rodents also feed upon these nutritious bulbs.

As yellow bells age, their petals turn a darker orange color to signal the end of their bloom season.

ORIGIN OF NAME

It is easy to see why these yellow bell-shaped flowers are called yellow bells. *Pudica* is Latin for "bashful," describing how this nodding flower shyly hides its face.

DOUBLE TAKE

Typically, one flower grows on each stem but, occasionally, you might see two.

CLOSED FOR THE SEASON

As yellow bells reach the end of their season, their petals turn a red-orange color and curl backward before withering away. This tells late-arriving pollinators that this flower has already been pollinated.

SIGNS OF SPRING

In 1806, after a harsh winter, explorers Lewis and Clark, eager to cross through the Rocky Mountains, found relief in the sight of yellow bells blooming—a welcome sign of spring.

Glacier-lily

Erythronium grandiflorum

WARNING!
This plant is toxic—do not eat.

FAMILY
Lily (Liliaceae)

NICKNAMES
yellow avalanche lily, yellow fawn-lily

BLOOM SEASON
March–August

HABITAT
open forest, clearings, and meadows, from low to high elevations

HEIGHT
6–12"

SUN TOLERANCE
full sun, part shade

POLLINATORS
bees

Meet Glacier-lily: Glacier-lilies' bright, lemon-yellow petals, gracefully emerging through melted snowbanks, are a welcome sign of spring. Early season bees, primarily queen bumblebees, also delight in their return. The yellow glacier-lily, with its dramatically curled petals, is easily confused with its close relatives: the white avalanche lily and the cream-colored Oregon fawn-lily. Many lily species exist in this region, so look for others as you explore. Never eat any part of a wild plant unless you're 100 percent certain of its identification and how to consume it safely.

ORIGIN OF NAME

This flower is called glacier-lily because it grows at the edges of melting snowbanks. Explorers Lewis and Clark relied on its bloom to indicate the start of spring.

PUZZLING PETALS

Lilies do not have petals. They have tepals, outer parts of the flower that look like petals.

FOOD FOR THE FOUR-LEGGED

Bears, big-horned sheep, deer, and elk eat the green seedpods and underground bulbs of this plant. Ground squirrels, gophers, and other rodents dig bulbs for winter food storage.

BULBS FOR BREAKFAST

Indigenous Americans relied on the deep-rooted bulbs of the glacier-lily for food. These nutritious bulbs were eaten raw, boiled for stews, and dried and stored for winter.

Arrow-leaf Buckwheat

Eriogonum compositum

FAMILY
Buckwheat (Polygonaceae)

NICKNAMES
heartleaf buck-wheat, northern buckwheat

BLOOM SEASON
May–July

HABITAT
dry, open areas, cliffs, and rocky slopes, from low to high elevations

HEIGHT
8–30"

SUN TOLERANCE
full sun

POLLINATORS
bees, beetles, butterflies, flies, wasps

Meet Arrow-leaf Buckwheat: Arrow-leaf buckwheat attracts many pollinator species but is especially important to butterflies. At least a dozen butterfly species rely on buckwheat, including blue, copper, and hairstreak butterflies. Buds and leaves make great food for young caterpillars, and adult butterflies rely on the plant's nourishing nectar. Arrow-leaf buckwheat also serves as a reliable host plant during butterfly mating season. Check out the cheerful white-yellow flowers growing in umbrella-shaped clusters called umbels. Doesn't it make sense that a flower with that many tiny blossoms would be a pollinator favorite?

ORIGIN OF NAME

The Greek words *erion*, meaning "wool," and *gonu*, meaning "knee or joint," attempt to describe this wooly plant with bent stems.

LEAFING CLUES

Leaves can be great clues for identification. This plant has large, heart-shaped leaves that look like arrowheads. The top of the leaf is smooth and green whereas the underside is fuzzy and white.

CHILD'S PLAY

Colville-Okanagan children played games using buckwheat stems. Breaking off the main stem revealed a hook shape. They connected their stems, pulling until one child had the last unbroken stem, declaring them the winner.

PEST CONTROL

This wildflower helps its surrounding environment by attracting native bees and helpful insects that prey upon unwanted pests.

Broadleaf Stonecrop

Sedum spathulifolium

WARNING!
All parts of this plant are poisonous—do not eat.

FAMILY
Stonecrop (Crassulaceae)

NICKNAMES
spatula-leaf stonecrop

BLOOM SEASON
April–June

HABITAT
balds, coastal cliffs, ledges, and gravelly soil at middle elevations

HEIGHT	SUN TOLERANCE	POLLINATORS
2–8"	full sun	bees, flies

Meet Broadleaf Stonecrop: Pacific Northwest tribes including the Nuxalk Nation, Penelakut First Nations, Colville-Okanagan, Songhees, and Thompson used stonecrop to make medicines particularly helpful to mothers and children. Pregnant women chewed the leaves during their ninth month of pregnancy to help prepare for childbirth and milk production. The stalks were boiled to make medicine to ease pains during childbirth. Mothers treated children's wounds by squeezing juice from the leaves and stalks on their injuries. The plant also made a calming body wash to soothe nervous babies and medicine for treating children's stomachaches.

ORIGIN OF NAME

Spathulifolium relates to the word *spatula*, referring to the plant's spatula-shaped leaves, which are flat, broad, and widest at the end.

FAMILY NAME

As the family name hints, stonecrop often grows in places with rocks and *stones*.

WHAT'S A SUCCULENT?

Stonecrop is a succulent—a plant with thick, fleshy leaves and stems that can hold water easily. In Latin, *sucus* means "juice or sap."

LEAFING CLUES

This wildflower has lush leaves coated with a waxy blue finish that can store water easily. Its leaves grow in little rosettes with larger gray, sage-green, and red outer leaves.

Desert Parsley

Lomatium papilioniferum

FAMILY
Umbel/Parsley (Apiaceae)

NICKNAMES
biscuitroot, pungent desert parsley

BLOOM SEASON
April–June

HABITAT
dry, open, rocky places, from low to middle elevations

HEIGHT
6–24"

SUN TOLERANCE
full sun

POLLINATORS
bees, beetles, butterflies, flies, wasps

Meet Desert Parsley: Desert parsley is a crucial host plant for the rare Indra Swallowtail butterfly. While fluttering in mid-air, females deposit up to 30 eggs on the underside of the leaves. About a week later, the eggs hatch and the leaves feed the butterfly larvae. Pupae continue to live on the same plant for up to two years, but, unfortunately, desert parsley is one of the only plants for this rare butterfly. If you want to help the Indra Swallowtail butterfly and other pollinators, plant desert parsley in a sunny spot in your garden.

ORIGIN OF NAME
Indigenous Americans cooked the roots and ground them into flour, which they shaped into cakes or biscuits. This explains why this wildflower is also commonly called biscuitroot.

YUCK OR YUM?
While we might find its pungent odor unpleasant, flies prefer this foul-smelling flower. As we commonly see flies in other stinky places, like garbage and animal remains, it is not surprising they are attracted to strong-smelling flowers too.

FAMILIAR FOOD
Do these soft, green, fern-like leaves remind you of any foods you eat? Carrot tops? Parsley? Dill? That's because they're all part of the same plant family.

SMART DESIGN
The flowers bloom close to the ground for warmth. Then, the stems grow taller as the seeds ripen, providing an advantage for accessing sunlight and a leg up for spreading its seeds farther away.

Western Buttercup

Ranunculus occidentalis

WARNING! This plant is poisonous—do not eat.

FAMILY
Buttercup (Ranunculaceae)

NICKNAMES
western field buttercup

BLOOM SEASON
April–June

HABITAT
moist to well-drained soil, from low to middle elevations

HEIGHT	SUN TOLERANCE	POLLINATORS
8–18"	full sun, part shade	bees, beetles, butterflies, flies

Meet Western Buttercup: The Indigenous American Aleut Tribe used buttercup juice to poison the tips of their arrows. And, despite being poisonous, buttercups are important to many animals. Birds, ducks, and wild turkeys eat their seeds; deer, muskrats, and skunks eat their leaves and stems. Buttercups are also important for many pollinators, especially early season pollinators. They have a unique pool of nectar at the bottom of their petals, which attracts insects to help with pollination. Their early spring arrival was helpful for the Shasta people, as the blooms foretold that the salmon run would begin soon.

ORIGIN OF NAME

In Latin, *ranunculus* means "little frog." Although western buttercups look nothing like little frogs, they do grow in damp areas where frogs are often found.

SUN CHASER

This flower is heliotropic, meaning its petals turn to follow the sun's path throughout the day.

DRAWN TO THE LIGHT

Did you notice that buttercup petals shine? They are covered with a glossy starch layer. When the sun hits the petals, the reflective properties create a bright flash of light, which attracts pollinators from a distance.

COWS AND BUTTERCUPS

People once believed that butter got its rich yellow color from cows eating buttercups, but buttercups are poisonous to cows. A cow who eats buttercups will produce bitter-tasting, reddish colored milk.

Monkey-flower

Erythranthe guttata

FAMILY
Lopseed (Phrymaceae)

NICKNAMES
seep-spring monkey-flower

BLOOM SEASON
March–September

HABITAT
wet places, from low to middle elevations

HEIGHT
3–30″

SUN TOLERANCE
full sun, part shade

POLLINATORS
bees

Meet Monkey-flower: Monkey-flowers are symmetrical, meaning their left and right sides mirror each other and will line up nearly perfectly when folded together along an imaginary centerline. Monkey-flowers have five petals that join at their bases to form two lobes—curved parts where the petals are unattached. Two smaller smooth petals form the upper lobe, and the bottom lobe consists of three hairy petals with reddish brown spots. In addition to being decorative, these spots also serve an important function for pollination, guiding bees to the landing spot for gathering pollen and nectar.

ORIGIN OF NAME

Before 2012, this flower was in the genus *Mimulus*, Latin for "to mime or look like," because many people think these unusually shaped flowers resemble monkey faces. What do you think?

PLEASE PASS THE SALT

Monkey-flower leaves absorb salt from the soil easily, making them a great salt substitute.

BLOOM ON

Monkey-flowers will bloom all summer as long as they get enough moisture. Look for them in wet places near seeps, springs, ponds, and small streams.

FLOWER MEDICINE

Indigenous Americans used the flowers to brew a tea to treat stomachaches, the leaves and stems to make steam baths to relieve sore chests and back aches, and the roots and flowers to make bandages.

Gold-star

Crocidium multicaule

FAMILY
Composite/Aster (Asteraceae)

NICKNAMES
spring gold

BLOOM SEASON
February–June

HABITAT
open grasslands and sandy soils, from low to middle elevations

HEIGHT
2–8"

SUN TOLERANCE
full sun

POLLINATORS
bees, beetles, flies, wasps

Meet Gold-star: Gold-star is among the first wildflowers to bloom in spring, bringing a delightful burst of cheerful lemon-yellow color after months of winter white. These flowers grow together closely in dry open spaces, creating a golden carpet on the forest floor. Several small yellow wildflowers bloom at this time, making it easy to confuse them for gold-stars. A handy trick to help you identify these lovely flowers accurately is that gold-stars are about the size of a dime—bring one along for size comparison when exploring.

ORIGIN OF NAME

The Greek word *crocidium* means "tufts." Look closely, and you will see fluffy tufts of tiny hairs growing just above where the leaves connect to the stems.

SAGEBRUSH STARS

Gold-stars grow in many habitats, from low to middle elevations, but are especially common in areas where sagebrush is found.

SEED OR FRUIT?

The part of this plant that most people think of as its seed is actually an achene, a fruit holding the seed. Gold-star achenes are brown and fuzzy and become gluey when wet.

CURIOUS COMPOSITES

Gold-stars are composite flowers, which means they are made up of many tiny flowers called florets. When all these parts are viewed together, they appear as one big flower.

Oregon Sunshine

Eriophyllum lanatum

FAMILY
Composite/Aster (Asteraceae)

NICKNAMES
woolly sunflower

BLOOM SEASON
May–August

HABITAT
dry, open, often rocky areas, from low to high elevations

HEIGHT
4–40"

SUN TOLERANCE
full sun

POLLINATORS
bees, beetles, butterflies, flies, moths

Meet Oregon Sunshine: This resilient native sunflower is deer-resistant and quick to grow, making it perfect for replanting disturbed areas after fires and excavation. Oregon sunshine is drought-resistant, which allows it to thrive in dry, harsh places where many other plants cannot. Its leaves and stems are covered in little hairs called trichomes that help the plant conserve water by reflecting heat and reducing how much dry air can blow across the leaf's surface, which minimizes evaporation. Oregon sunshine needs water only once a month. In fact, too much water will kill it.

ORIGIN OF NAME

Eriophyllum **comes from the Greek word *erion*, which means "wool," and *phyllon*, which means "leaf." *Lanatum* is Latin for "covered with long woolly hair," the reason behind its nickname woolly sunflower.**

HEALTH BENEFITS

The Upper Skagit people rubbed the leaves on their skin during cold weather to prevent sore, rough, cracked skin. The Miwok people used leaves to make a bandage to apply to aching body parts.

LEGENDS OF LOVE

Looking for love advice? The Chehalis people dried these flowers to use as love charms.

PREPARED FOR POLLINATORS

Oregon sunshine's beckoning yellow flowers are flat and up to 2 inches wide, making an ideal landing pad for pollinators looking to access nectar and pollen.

Arrowleaf Balsamroot

Balsamorhiza sagittata

FAMILY
Composite/Aster (Asteraceae)

NICKNAMES
breadroot, spring sunflower

BLOOM SEASON
April–July

HABITAT
grasslands, shrub-steppe, and other open areas, from low to middle elevations

HEIGHT
8–36"

SUN TOLERANCE
full sun

POLLINATORS
bees, beetles, bumblebees, butterflies, flies, and wasps

Meet Arrowleaf Balsamroot: Indigenous Americans used nearly every part of this plant for food. They peeled the stems and ate them raw and steamed and pit-baked the roots and young shoots. The large arrow-shaped leaves could be eaten raw but were frequently wrapped around camas bulbs, then roasted. The nutritious, oil-rich seeds were eaten raw or ground into flour for making bread and cakes. Lastly, they boiled roots to drink as a coffee-like beverage. Never eat any part of a wild plant unless you're 100 percent certain of its identification and how to consume it safely.

ORIGIN OF NAME

As you may have guessed, arrowleaf balsamroot is named after its arrow-shaped leaves. *Balsam* refers to the sticky, sap-like substance covering the roots, which Indigenous Americans used to clean and heal minor wounds.

ROOTED TO REGROW

These cheery yellow flowers have deep taproots that can be as wide as a human wrist. This hardy taproot helps the plant regrow after being grazed by deer or burned in a fire.

WHEN NATURE CALLS

Arrowleaf balsamroot's leaves are large, fuzzy, and velvety soft, making them handy for use as toilet paper in nature. But beware, other species of balsamroot have spiny leaves. So, choose your wipes wisely.

SCENT SENSE

Take a good sniff of a balsamroot flower. What do you smell? Many say their roots smell like pine sap and their blossoms like chocolate.

ORANGE

California poppy, the state flower of California, is native along the Pacific Coast from Western Oregon to Baja, California.

Columbia Lily

Lilium columbianum

FAMILY
Lily (Liliaceae)

NICKNAMES
tiger lily

BLOOM SEASON
May–August

HABITAT
forest edges and openings, meadows, and prairies, from low to high elevations

HEIGHT
24–48"

SUN TOLERANCE
full sun, part shade

POLLINATORS
bees, hummingbirds, moths

Meet Columbia Lily: Columbia lily bulbs were a staple food for Indigenous people who ate them raw, boiled, or steamed—often with salmon roe or wild-game meat. They also dried them in underground earthen ovens to make a sweet, peppery cooking spice. The Colville-Okanagan people mixed dried bulbs and mashed stinkbugs into a powder to protect against witchcraft. Also spiritually significant in Indigenous American culture, Columbia lily represents harmony and balance with nature. Never eat any part of a wild plant unless you're 100 percent certain of its identification and how to consume it safely.

ORIGIN OF NAME

Lilium comes from the Greek word *lirion*, meaning "white lily." Clearly, this lily is not white. Instead, its vibrant orange color resembles a tiger, inspiring its nickname, tiger lily.

KEEP AWAY, CATS

Keep your cats away from this lily. Its pollen is toxic to cats and can cause sleepiness and vomiting.

FLOWER OF FORTUNE

In Chinese culture, a lily symbolizes wealth, prosperity, and good fortune and is often given as a gift for celebrations.

LOCAL HERO

The Columbia lily plays a key role in supporting local ecosystems and promoting biodiversity by attracting many kinds of pollinators.

California Poppy

Eschscholzia californica

FAMILY
Poppy
(Papaveraceae)

NICKNAMES
California sunshine, cups of gold, golden poppy

BLOOM SEASON
May–September

HABITAT
ditches, meadows, open areas, parks, and roadsides, at low elevation

HEIGHT
6–16"

SUN TOLERANCE
full sun

POLLINATORS
bees, beetles, bumblebees, self-pollination

Meet California Poppy: California poppy has four shiny, round petals. These silky golden petals are pretty as well as particular and peculiar. Nicknamed "California sunshine," the flower radiates brightly all day, but when night falls and temperatures drop, it closes tightly to protect itself—and will remain closed the next day if it doesn't like the weather. These fair-weather flowers dislike it too cold, cloudy, or windy. Interestingly, the petals' color varies depending on where the plant grows—California poppies growing closer to the coast have golden petals with orange interiors, whereas those growing farther inland bloom orange.

ORIGIN OF NAME

Although these wildflowers grow abundantly throughout the Pacific Northwest, they are most popular in California. In 1903, California named them the state flower and, every year, on April 6, Californians celebrate California Poppy Day.

SUPER SEEDS

California poppies self-seed and can remain active in healthy soil for up to eight years, making them easy to cultivate or grow. Their seeds are also useful in baking and cooking.

CURES FOR KIDS

Indigenous American parents commonly laid beautiful California poppy petals under their children's beds to help them sleep. They also rubbed the silky petals into children's hair to kill lice.

WILDFLOWER OR WEED?

California poppies are considered native (originally and naturally growing) in California and Oregon. In Washington state, however, they are considered invasive weeds that make it difficult for native plants to grow there.

California poppies close up for protection when it's too cold, cloudy, or windy.

PINK TO RED TO PURPLE

Poet's shooting stars welcome hikers at the Lookout Mountain Trailhead.

Sagebrush Mariposa Lily

Calochortus macrocarpus

FAMILY
Lily (Liliaceae)

NICKNAMES
green-banded star-tulip

BLOOM SEASON
May–July

HABITAT
dry open forests, grasslands, hillsides, and sagebrush, from low to middle elevations

HEIGHT
8–23"

SUN TOLERANCE
full sun

POLLINATORS
bees, beetles

Meet Sagebrush Mariposa Lily: Bearing up to five blooms and growing up to 20 inches tall, one tiny underground bulb supports this plant. Each petal's exterior is marked with a center green stripe; inside, a darker purple line encircles the yellow center. Soft, tiny hairs cover the three petals above the base. The three narrow, pointed sepals (longer than the petals) hold and protect the unopened flower bud. After blooming, these sepals lie decoratively alongside the petals. Never eat any part of a wild plant unless you're 100 percent certain of its identification and how to consume it safely.

ORIGIN OF NAME

Calochortus comes from two Greek words: *kalos*, meaning "beautiful," and *chortos*, meaning "grass."

SUN WORSHIPPER

This lily needs very little water and can live in hot, dry conditions and on rocky outcrops where other plants cannot.

PRINCIPLE FOOD

The carrot-shaped bulbs were important food for many Indigenous people who ate them raw, boiled, or roasted. In spring, the sweet buds were a tasty treat before they bloomed.

CAT CLUES

Rub the inside of these triangular-shaped petals. Can you guess why a close relative of this flower is called cat's ears?

Bleeding Heart

Dicentra formosa

FAMILY
Poppy (Papaveraceae)

NICKNAMES
Pacific bleeding heart

BLOOM SEASON
April–June

HABITAT
moist woods, from low to middle elevations

HEIGHT
6–20"

SUN TOLERANCE
shade

POLLINATORS
bees, birds, butterflies

Meet Bleeding Heart: These delicate heart-shaped flowers carry the legend of a lovestruck prince who failed to win the heart of his beloved princess. Heartbroken, he plunged a dagger into his heart and, the story goes, in the exact place he died, the first bleeding heart grew. While wandering shaded forests in spring, look for clusters of pink hearts hanging above waxy, bluish-green leaves. For each heart-shaped flower you see, give thanks to someone you're grateful for. Never eat any part of a wild plant unless you're 100 percent certain of its identification and how to consume it safely.

ORIGIN OF NAME

This flower's common name comes from its heart-shaped flowers with flared tips. *Dicentra* refers to the two nectar-bearing spurs, and *formosa* means "beautiful."

PURPOSEFUL PLANTS

The Upper Skagit people made a hair wash from crushed plants and leaves. They also chewed roots to ease toothache pain and pounded roots to make medicines.

ANT APPRECIATION

The plant's tiny black seeds have an oil-rich part that ants feed to their young. After feeding, they discard the unwanted parts of the seed, unknowingly replanting it.

GARDEN FAVORITE

If your garden is in a neighborhood shared with rabbits and deer, you'll be glad to know these critters do not enjoy the flavor of bleeding hearts. So, plant away.

Fireweed

Chamerion angustifolium

FAMILY
Evening Primrose (Onagraceae)

NICKNAMES
blooming Sally, rosebay willowherb

BLOOM SEASON
May–September

HABITAT
open or disturbed sites, especially recent burns, in clear-cuts, meadows, and mixed forests, from low to high elevations

HEIGHT
24–60"

SUN TOLERANCE
full sun

POLLINATORS
bees, butterflies, hummingbirds, moths

Meet Fireweed: In early spring, before blooming, fireweed's stems offered Indigenous Americans raw, juicy tissue as a sweet treat, or they were boiled or steamed like asparagus. Canadian First Nations people dried stem peelings and twisted them into thread-like twine to make fishing nets. The seed fluff, combined with dog and mountain-goat hair, was used for weaving and padding. A blend of fireweed and other native plants could treat skin conditions and help reduce inflammation. Never eat any part of a wild plant unless you're 100 percent certain of its identification and how to consume it safely.

ORIGIN OF NAME

This wildflower is known as fireweed because it grows . . . well . . . *like a weed* in places where fires have recently burned.

MOOSE MATING

Instead of using traditional calendars, the Cree people relied on the first bloom of fireweed to indicate the start of moose mating season.

FIREWEED FEASTS

Fireweed is a valuable food for wildlife, including caribou, cattle, deer, hares (wild rabbits), moose, and muskrats.

PECULIAR POLLEN

We usually think of pollen as yellow, but fireweed breaks the mold with its peculiar gray-colored pollen.

Bitterroot

Lewisia rediviva

FAMILY
Miner's Lettuce (Montiaceae)

NICKNAMES
none

BLOOM SEASON
April–June

HABITAT
gravelly slopes and rocky outcrops, from low to middle elevations

HEIGHT
1–3"

SUN TOLERANCE
full sun

POLLINATORS
bees, insects

Meet Bitterroot: A short wildflower with a long list of interesting facts. Indigenous Americans called it *spetlem*, meaning "hand peeled," and *mo'ôtáa-heséeo'ôtse*, meaning "black medicine." In 1806, the Shoshone people gave it as food to the Lewis and Clark expedition explorers. The name doesn't lie—bitterroot has bitter-tasting roots, so they were typically cooked with meat or berries to improve the flavor. French trappers later agreed, and called it *racine amère*, or bitter root. In 1895, Montana chose bitterroot as its state flower and named three major geological features after it: the Bitterroot Mountains, Bitterroot Valley, and Bitterroot River.

ORIGIN OF NAME

Lewisia refers to the explorer Meriwether Lewis, who dug up a bulb in 1806. Two years later, he planted the dried-up bulb, which grew again, earning it the name *rediviva*, meaning "restored to life."

POWER ROOTS

The Shoshone people believed the root's small red core contained special powers and could stop a bear from attacking.

BUSY BEES

Bitterroot blooms for only two to three days, so bees and insect pollinators must act quickly. If you want to see this beautiful bloom, look for it regularly during bloom season or you might miss it too.

WINTER PHOTOSYNTHESIS

In fall, a cluster of leaves grows up from the soil. All winter long, these leaves filter sunlight to photosynthesize and create food for new flowers in spring.

Twinflower

Linnaea borealis

FAMILY
Twinflower (Linnaeaceae)

NICKNAMES
American twin-flower, western twinflower

BLOOM SEASON
May–September

HABITAT
forest edges and open forests, from low to high elevations

HEIGHT
2–6"

SUN TOLERANCE
full shade, part shade

POLLINATORS
bumblebees, butterflies, insects

Meet Twinflower: This plant is appropriately named, given its twin-like structure. Look closely at the stems of this creeping evergreen vine, and you'll notice a distinct Y shape where pale pink, trumpet-shaped flowers grow together—like twins. The round, leathery leaves are twins too, growing in pairs on opposite sides of the stem. Twinflowers are semi-woody and evergreen. They spread easily across the ground, forming large mats of fragrant flowers. As long as they have at least some shade, twin-flowers grow in most ecosystems of the Pacific Northwest.

ORIGIN OF NAME

Linnaea honors Carl Linnaeus, a Swedish biologist who named nearly 8,000 plants in his lifetime. *Borealis* means "northern" and refers to the colder, northern regions where twinflowers thrive.

RISING CONCERNS

Twinflowers commonly grow in high-elevation habitats with cooler temperatures, making them a species of concern as Earth's temperatures increase.

FROZEN FLOWERS

During the Pleistocene era, also known as the Ice Age, twinflowers likely grew farther south than where they grow today. This was because, as southern regions warmed over time, many plants couldn't survive.

NATURAL MEDICINE

The Tanana people applied a bandage of twinflower leaves to treat headaches. The Snohomish used it to make a medicine to treat colds.

Poet's Shooting Star

Primula poetica

FAMILY
Primrose (Primulaceae)

NICKNAMES
Narcissus shooting star

BLOOM SEASON
March–May

HABITAT
drier woods near sources of water and grassy slopes that are wet in the spring at low elevation

HEIGHT
5–8"

SUN TOLERANCE
full sun, part shade

POLLINATORS
bees

Meet Poet's Shooting Star: Two unusual factors affect shooting stars' pollination. Unlike most wildflowers, it does not produce nectar. This alone discourages many pollinators from visiting. Furthermore, the petals' unique shape makes it difficult for most pollinators to access pollen. So, shooting stars must rely on specific pollen-foraging bees that use a special *buzz pollination* method: When a bee arrives at the flower, it uses its strong jaws to hang upside-down from the flower. It then buzzes its wings rapidly, causing the wildflower to vibrate, which releases and showers pollen onto the bee.

This bee hangs upside-down and buzzes its wings rapidly, causing the flower to vibrate and release pollen.

ORIGIN OF NAME

Until recently, this flower was in the *Dodecatheon* family, named after *dodecus*, Latin for 12, and *theos*, meaning "God." This name led people to believe the 12 major Greek gods protected it.

FEAR NO DEER

Don't fret about deer munching on this wildflower—poet's shooting star is considered deer-proof. These flowers go untouched by deer, likely because they don't like the taste.

WESTWARD, HO

According to legend, the black tips of these flowers always lean to the west. So, settlers traveling west may have used them to guide their way.

SHAPE MATTERS

The unique shape of this plant's flower affects how it reproduces (makes new plants). When it dies, its upright seed capsules release seeds in nearby soil, creating new plants for the next season.

Prairie Star

Lithophragma parviflorum

FAMILY
Saxifrage (Saxifragaceae)

NICKNAMES
woodland star

BLOOM SEASON
April–June

HABITAT
forest openings, prairies, and sagebrush desert, from low to middle elevations

HEIGHT
4–12"

SUN TOLERANCE
full sun, part shade

POLLINATORS
bees, butterflies, flies, moths

Meet Prairie Star: Prairie star attracts many different kinds of pollinators, each for different reasons. Butterflies and moths find the petals convenient landing spots, perfect for gathering nectar. Prairie star has a special relationship, called mutualism, with a moth species known as Greya moths (*Greya politella*), meaning that both species help one another survive. Greya moths pollinate prairie stars, ensuring they can grow new flowers next year. In exchange, prairie stars serve as a host plant, providing a place for Greya moths to rest, drink nectar, and lay their eggs.

ORIGIN OF NAME

Parviflorum means "small-flowered," a well-suited name considering each plant contains a cluster of up to 14 small flowers on each stem. Ironically, there are similar species with even smaller flowers.

COUNT CAREFULLY

Prairie stars appear to have more petals than they actually do. Look closely—there are only five petals, but each is divided into three lobes at the tip, giving the illusion of more.

STOP TO SNIFF

Prairie star's flowers are tiny, but their fragrance is not. Stop and smell—some say the pinker the flower, the more fragrant it is. You be the judge.

WILDLY INDEPENDENT

If pollinators are unavailable, prairie star can reproduce independently through apomixis without fertilization.

Long-leaf Phlox

Phlox longifolia

FAMILY
Phlox (Polemoniaceae)

NICKNAMES
none

BLOOM SEASON
April–June

HABITAT
ponderosa pine forest openings to sagebrush desert, from low to middle elevations

HEIGHT
4–20"

SUN TOLERANCE
full sun

POLLINATORS
butterflies, moths

Meet Long-leaf Phlox: The quarter-size flowers of this plant feature numerous pinkish white petals surrounding bright white centers with notched petals, all clustered on slender, woody stems. Long-leaf phlox spreads rapidly, creating a spectacular blanket of pale pink color across open hillsides. These abundant beauties held significant medicinal value for Indigenous Americans who used the roots to make medicine for body aches, colds, and stomachaches. The Shoshone, specifically, used the leaves to prepare remedies for skin problems.

ORIGIN OF NAME

The Greek word *phlox* means "flame." *Longifolia* comes from the Latin words *longus*, or "long," and *folium*, or "leaf."

SIPPING STRAWS

Look at the underside of phlox. All five petals come from one tube. Butterflies and moths are ideal pollinators because their long tongues can reach down into the tube to access the nectar.

ANIMAL NUTRITION

Rabbits, groundhogs, deer, and moth larvae rely on the foliage, or leaves, for food.

FOLLOW THE SCENT

On warm summer days, phlox attracts butterflies and moths with its sweet floral scent.

Scarlet Paintbrush

Castilleja miniata

FAMILY
Broomrape (Orobanchaceae)

NICKNAMES
common paintbrush, painted cup

BLOOM SEASON
May–September

HABITAT
widespread from coastal bluffs to mountain meadows and slopes, from low to high elevations

HEIGHT
12–24"

SUN TOLERANCE
full sun to part shade

POLLINATORS
bees, hummingbirds

Meet Scarlet Paintbrush: Scarlet paintbrush's common name comes from an Indigenous American legend about a boy who dreamed of painting a perfect sunset. He tried repeatedly but could not create the exact color he saw each evening. Frustrated, he called upon the Great Spirit for help, who responded by scattering paintbrushes throughout the landscape, which blossomed into beautiful plants with "petals" that appeared to be painted red. But—those painted parts weren't petals but bracts, or modified leaves. Never eat any part of a wild plant unless you're 100 percent certain of its identification and how to consume it safely.

ORIGIN OF NAME

Castilleja honors the Spanish botanist Domingo Castillejo. *Miniata* means "cinnabar," a red color, referring to the flowers, which appear to be painted red.

MEANT TO BE

Hummingbirds cannot resist the alluring red color, and their long, skinny beaks fit perfectly inside the tube-shaped flowers. In fact, hummingbirds love paintbrush flowers so much that they're often called hummingbird feeders.

PIRATE PAINTBRUSHES

Paintbrush roots aren't strong enough to absorb all the water and minerals they need. So, they attach their roots to the roots of other host plants to steal nutrients from them.

MULTIPURPOSE PLANT

Indigenous Pacific Northwest tribes soaked these plants in grease to make hair oil and used the red leaves to make natural dyes. Children sucked sweet nectar from the flowers for a treat.

Red Columbine

Aquilegia formosa

WARNING! Nearly all parts of this plant are poisonous and its seeds are deadly—do not eat.

FAMILY
Buttercup (Ranunculaceae)

NICKNAMES
western columbine, crimson columbine

BLOOM SEASON
May–August

HABITAT
lightly shaded open woods with loose soil, from low to middle elevations

HEIGHT
8–48"

SUN TOLERANCE
full sun to part shade

POLLINATORS
bees, hummingbirds, moths

Meet Red Columbine: Red, an uncommon color in nature, makes this wildflower special. Observe the nodding blossoms float and bob in the gentle breeze. Notice each drooping flower's inner yellow structure resembling a honeycomb—its only true petals—with five long, red, tube-like spurs behind it. These deep spurs challenge many pollinators who can't reach the nectar, but moths, hummingbirds, and butterflies are expert columbine pollinators, with their long mouthparts ideal for reaching deep inside blossoms. For the best view of this elaborate wildflower, lie on the ground and look up at the flower from underneath.

A native Anna's Hummingbird uses its long mouthpart to access nectar at the end of the tube-shaped flower.

ORIGIN OF NAME

Red columbine's scientific name accurately describes its impressive appearance—*aquila* means "eagle," which refers to its talon-like nectary, and *formosa* means "handsome," or "well-formed," which perfectly describes its elaborate honey-comb formation.

TRADITIONAL USES

Despite this plant being highly toxic, Indigenous Americans used the seeds and leaves medicinally to treat coughs, sore throats, and stomachaches.

LURING LOVE

Although it's nearly scentless, Indigenous Americans of the plateaus traditionally used this wildflower to make men's perfume. They also crushed the seeds to make love charms.

PILFERING POLLINATORS

Sneaky butterflies and stealthy bumblebees sometimes hover and steal sweet nectar without touching the flower. This is a problem because it means the columbine doesn't get pollinated and therefore won't reproduce.

Great Purple Monkey-flower

Erythranthe lewisii

FAMILY
Lopseed (Phrymaceae)

NICKNAMES
Lewis's monkey-flower

BLOOM SEASON
June–August

HABITAT
along rivers and streams and in wet meadows, from middle to high elevations and occasionally low elevations

HEIGHT	SUN TOLERANCE	POLLINATORS
12–48"	full sun	hummingbirds

Meet Great Purple Monkey-flower: More than 100 species of monkey-flowers grow worldwide. Most have bright yellow flowers, making the large, magenta flowers of *Erythranthe lewisii* easy to spot and identify. Most of its yellow cousins are annuals, requiring replanting each year from seed, but the perennial great purple monkey-flower regrows on its own yearly. Most species of monkey-flowers are bee-pollinated, but as bees can't see red, they typically don't bother with these red-purple blossoms. Hummingbirds, however, love to visit these bright, tubular flowers and appreciate not having to compete with bee swarms to do so.

ORIGIN OF NAME

Lewisii honors explorer Meriwether Lewis, who collected hundreds of plant specimens on his travels along the Oregon Trail with William Clark.

TRACING THE TRAIL

According to their journals, Lewis and Clark first encountered this cheerful flower at the headwaters of the Missouri River in what is known today as Trail Creek, Montana.

NAMES CHANGE

A wildflower's scientific name can change as botanists discover new information. Until recently, this wildflower was classified as *Mimulus lewisii*, so keep an eye out for this alias in older field guides.

MONKEY FACE

The center of this flower resembles a smiling monkey, explaining its common name, monkey-flower.

Scarlet Gilia

Ipomopsis aggregata

FAMILY
Phlox (Polemoniaceae)

NICKNAMES
skyrocket

BLOOM SEASON
May–August

HABITAT
open or lightly wooded, drier meadows and rocky slopes, from low to high elevations

HEIGHT
12–48"

SUN TOLERANCE
full sun

POLLINATORS
hummingbirds

Meet Scarlet Gilia: Found mainly east of the Cascades, scarlet gilia boasts long, orange-red, tube-shaped flowers that open into five speckled petals. Hummingbirds love these flowers, reaching inside with their long beaks for sweet nectar. In Oregon, children of the Klamath Tribes would suck nectar from the flowers for a sugary snack. Elk, mule deer, and other herbivores like to eat the leaves. But don't worry—after their feast, the plant grows back even stronger. Never eat any part of a wild plant unless you're 100 percent certain of its identification and how to consume it safely.

ORIGIN OF NAME

Named after Italian scientist Filippo Luigi Gilii, this wildflower has an Italian pronunciation: *gee-lee-uh*. Originally, this plant was a member of the genus *Gillia*.

WINTER WARMTH

This plant's fernlike leaves grow low to the ground, helping keep it warm in colder temperatures.

POLLINATION INVESTIGATION

Currently, scientists use this plant to track pollinating hummingbirds and better understand their pollination techniques.

BEAUTY'S SECRET

This plant's stunning blossoms hide the fact that its leaves have an unpleasant, skunky odor.

Showy Milkweed

Asclepias speciosa

WARNING! This plant contains harmful toxins—do not touch.

FAMILY
Milkweed (Asclepiadoideae)

NICKNAMES
butterfly flower, butterfly weed

BLOOM SEASON
June–August

HABITAT
seasonally wet irrigation ditches, roadsides, and riverbanks at low elevations

HEIGHT
18–50"

SUN TOLERANCE
full sun

POLLINATORS
bees, beetles, butterflies, wasps

Meet Showy Milkweed: Although its name contains the word *weed*, and it's sometimes treated as one, milkweed is not a weed. Showy milkweed is critical to the survival of the endangered Monarch butterfly. You may know these orange, winged marvels, famous for their impressive migration from the northern United States and southern Canada to Mexico and California, 3,000 miles south, to winter. Milkweed is the only food source for Monarch caterpillars. It also provides a habitat for them to live and raise their young. Help these endangered butterflies by planting milkweed and teaching others why it is important.

ORIGIN OF NAME

Milkweed gets its name from the milky white sap that oozes from the plant when it is cut. This sap protects the flower from hungry herbivores—but don't get it on your skin or in your eyes. It will hurt.

DESIGNED TO FLY

Milkweed has teardrop-shaped seedpods that split open and release light, fluffy seeds into the wind, blowing them to new locations where future plants can grow.

BEE HELPFUL

Milkweed attracts many bumblebees, honeybees, and native bees, all essential pollinators who need our help to survive.

USEFUL FIBERS

Indigenous Americans used the strong fibers of milkweed plants to make ropes and nets.

Grass Widow

Olsynium douglasii

FAMILY
Iris (Iridaceae)

NICKNAMES
purple-eyed grass widow, satin flower

BLOOM SEASON
February–March

HABITAT
rocky open fields and meadows that are wet in spring, from low to middle elevations

HEIGHT
6–12"

SUN TOLERANCE
part sun

POLLINATORS
bees

Meet Grass Widow: This species is the only member of the *Olsynium* genus native to North America; all others grow in South America. It's widespread in the Pacific Northwest, especially the Cascade Range's eastern side. Fascinatingly, these wildflowers look different depending on which side of the mountains they grow. West of the range, they display darker reddish-purple tepals with usually one or two flowers per stem. Those on the eastern side flaunt lighter pinkish-purple tepals with two to three flowers per stem. Pay attention to the appearance of the grass widows you find and note where they grow.

ORIGIN OF NAME

In nineteeth-century colonial India, British wives typically spent hot summers living at higher, cooler elevations, while their husbands worked in lower, drier lands. These women were called *grass widows*. Pacific Northwest settlers, seeing wildflowers blooming at higher elevations, likely confused the stories of the women in India with Native American women (commonly referred to then as *Indians*) and named the flowers accordingly. This delicate flower's soft, silky petals give it the nickname satin flower.

FLOWERS AND FIR TREES

David Douglas was the first botanist to officially record a grass widow, in 1826 in Oregon near Celilo Falls. He is also the namesake for the famous Douglas firs all over the Pacific Northwest.

FIRST TO BLOOM

As soon as the snow melts, grass widow pops up all over the Pacific Northwest, providing a welcome burst of color and reminding us spring is coming.

Taper-tip Onion

Allium acuminatum

WARNING!
All parts of this plant can be toxic—do not eat.

FAMILY
Amaryllis (Amaryllidaceae)

NICKNAMES
Hooker's onion

BLOOM SEASON
May–July

HABITAT
open areas, including balds, dry slopes, grasslands, and rocky outcroppings, from low to middle elevations

HEIGHT
4–14"

SUN TOLERANCE
full sun, part shade

POLLINATORS
bees, bumblebees, flies, hummingbirds

Meet Taper-tip Onion: As its name suggests, this wildflower is an onion and grows from an underground bulb that stores energy for the plant's future use. Although Indigenous Americans ate taper-tip onions, please note that all the plant's parts contain varying toxicity levels, making them unsafe to eat. Indigenous tribes harvested and cooked these bulbs in open pits or dried them for seasoning. A clue to correctly identifying this plant is its onion- or garlic-like scent. Never eat any part of a wild plant unless you're 100 percent certain of its identification and how to consume it safely.

Taper-tip onions produce a small underground bulb that smells like, well, an onion.

ORIGIN OF NAME
Acuminatum comes from the Latin word *acumin*, meaning "to curve or taper out," which describes the tapered shape at the tips of this flower's petals.

WESTWARD REPRESENTATION
This plant grows in every state west of the Rocky Mountains.

COLORFUL CLUSTERS
Each stem can have a cluster of flowers (umbel) with up to 40 pink-purple blooms.

BARE STEM BLOOMER
Before the flower blooms, its long, grooved leaves wither and die, leaving behind a bare stem to support the future blossoms.

VIOLET TO BLUE

Camas blankets a field near Camas, Washington.

Camas

Camassia quamash

FAMILY
Lily (Liliaceae)

NICKNAMES
blue camas, common quamash

BLOOM SEASON
April–June

HABITAT
open, moist areas, often dry by late spring, from low to middle elevations

HEIGHT
12–24"

SUN TOLERANCE
full sun, part shade

POLLINATORS
bees, beetles, butterflies, flies, wasps

Meet Camas: Camas are considered a cultural keystone species because their crisp, starchy underground bulbs were an important food for Indigenous Americans. Bulbs were eaten raw, or steamed in earthen ovens until browned, soft, and sweet. Once sun-dried, they were ground into flour or pressed into bricks and stored for winter. Lewis and Clark recorded that the Nez Perce people saved their expedition from starvation by sharing camas bulbs with them. Never eat any part of a wild plant unless you're 100 percent certain of its identification and how to consume it safely.

ORIGIN OF NAME

The name *camas* comes from the Indigenous Nootka people of the Pacific Northwest's word *chamas*, which means "sweet." Can you guess why?

PATIENCE PAYS OFF

A camas plant can take several years to bloom, but your patience will be rewarded when you finally see its spectacular flowers.

COLOR CLUES

Camas blossoms growing closer to the coast are typically a darker purple color, whereas those growing farther inland tend to be lighter blue in color.

LANDMARK NAMES

Camas, Washington, and Lacamas Lake, near Vancouver, Washington were named after this important native wildflower.

Rocky Mountain Iris

Iris missouriensis

WARNING!
This plant contains a poison called irisine—do not eat.

FAMILY
Iris (Iridaceae)

NICKNAMES
western blue flag

BLOOM SEASON
May–July

HABITAT
meadows that are wet in spring, especially in sagebrush and ponderosa pine forests, low to high elevations

HEIGHT
8–24"

SUN TOLERANCE
part shade

POLLINATORS
bees, flies, hummingbirds

Meet Rocky Mountain Iris: Although these plants contain a poison called irisine, Indigenous Americans carefully and skillfully learned to use them for many important purposes. Numerous tribes constructed strong, flexible cords from its leaves and stems. The cords were woven into fishing nets or used as hunting ropes designed to catch deer and other wild game. The Klamath Tribes in Oregon made traditional plant medicines with this wildflower, intended to treat ailments including bladder infections, earaches, kidney troubles, and toothaches. Additionally, many tribes used these beautiful flowers as decorations for special ceremonies.

ORIGIN OF NAME

In Greek mythology, Iris, the goddess of rainbows, was a messenger for the gods, and wherever she stepped, beautiful flowers sprouted.

NECTAR GUIDES

Besides being decorative, the white and yellow veins on the petals help guide pollinating insects to the nectar.

SEEING DOUBLES

Irises appear to have six petals, but the three upright blue parts are the only true petals. The lower drooping parts are sepals designed to protect the flower.

WILDFLOWER OR WEED?

This flower tastes bitter to cows and spreads rapidly in pastures. Some ranchers consider it a problematic weed whereas others see it as a wildflower threatened by human activities and in need of protection.

Early Blue Violet

Viola adunca

FAMILY
Violet (Violaceae)

NICKNAMES
hook violet, wild dog violet

BLOOM SEASON
April–August

HABITAT
dry to moist meadows and open woods, from low to high elevations

HEIGHT
1–4"

SUN TOLERANCE
full sun

POLLINATORS
bees, bumblebees, flies

Meet Early Blue Violet: Although tiny, its role in our ecosystem is enormous because it hosts the larvae of many butterfly and moth species, including Myrtle's Silverspot butterfly, which is in danger of becoming extinct (disappearing permanently). Special working dogs are trained to smell and locate Myrtle's Silverspot caterpillar poop—the amount they find helps determine how many butterflies live in an area, which areas are popular for feeding, and where protection is needed. These helpful dogs also inspired this wildflower's nickname: wild dog violet.

ORIGIN OF NAME

Adunca means "hook" and refers to the curved spurs at the tips of the flower's two outer petals.

SOARING SEEDS

When early blue violet's seedpods are mature, they burst open and seeds shoot out explosively. Mice and birds eat some seeds, while others take root in the soil for next year.

NATIVE USES

Indigenous Americans of the Blackfoot, Dakelh, Klallam, Makah, and Tolowa Tribes used the roots and leaves for medicine and the petals to make a blue dye to paint their arrows.

BEE BENEFITS

To a bee's keen eyes, the striped veins on the petals shine ultraviolet, creating a glowing map that guides them straight to the sweet nectar.

Shrub Penstemon

Penstemon fruticosus

FAMILY
Figwort (Scrophulariaceae)

NICKNAMES
beardtongue, bush penstemon

BLOOM SEASON
May–September

HABITAT
rocky, open to wooded areas, from low to high elevations

HEIGHT
12–24″

SUN TOLERANCE
full sun

POLLINATORS
bees, bumblebees, flies, hummingbirds, wasps

Meet Shrub Penstemon: More than 250 penstemon varieties exist; over 80 are native to the Pacific Northwest, meaning originally from there. Penstemons, with their shrub-like woody bases, are different from many wildflowers. These bushes of purple-blue flowers grow in spirals, each with five irregular petals. The lower lip of the petal configuration is bearded with long, white hairs. Their sword-shaped leaves, with sharp, pointed teeth, grow in an alternating pattern. Their long stems create a net-like structure that holds the soil in place firmly—handy, because penstemons grow in rocky, exposed areas where soil erosion can be problematic.

ORIGIN OF NAME

The scientific name consists of the Latin words *penta*, meaning "five," and *stamon*, meaning "stamen." Next time you see a penstemon, feel free to check the math.

WILDLIFE CONNECTIONS

Penstemon is a favorite food source for antelope, deer, and wild birds. The plant's bush-like shape provides shelter for small birds.

FAILED LOVE ATTEMPTS

Using a love potion is a brilliant idea—unless, of course, something goes wrong. In those unlucky cases, the Iroquois knew how to use penstemon to cure a failed love potion.

HAPPY FEET

Indigenous Americans living near the Pacific Ocean lined the insides of their moccasins with penstemon leaves for added comfort.

Small-flowered Blue-eyed Mary

Collinsia parviflora

FAMILY
Plantain (Plantaginaceae)

NICKNAMES
collinsia

BLOOM SEASON
March–July

HABITAT
places that are moist in spring, from low to high elevations

HEIGHT
2–12"

SUN TOLERANCE
full sun

POLLINATORS
bees, beetles, flies, wasps

Meet Blue-eyed Mary: When you find a blue-eyed Mary, look closely at the leaves. Do you see tiny purple spots? Scientists in British Columbia observed that just some blue-eyed Marys have spotted leaves, and those plants usually grow in areas with cool temperatures. Scientists discovered that the spots tend to disappear within days when the spotted-leaved plants are moved from outside (cooler temperatures) to greenhouses with warmer temperatures. Scientists wonder if these spots help the plant absorb sunlight, to warm the leaves and increase the plant's rate of photosynthesis (how it makes its food from the sun).

ORIGIN OF NAME

Blue-eyed Mary's name comes from the beautiful blue petals fused together that open up to resemble a face.

OFF TO THE RACES

Navajo people once believed this plant was a good-luck charm to help a horse run fast.

TINY BUT MIGHTY

Despite its size, this small wildflower plays a huge role as a food source for the larvae of the endangered Taylor's checkerspot butterfly.

LURING PROTECTION

This flower has pockets of nectar called nectaries that attract ants. While eating sweet nectar, ants unknowingly protect the plant from hungry herbivores who don't want to eat a plant infested with ants.

Bluebell

Campanula rotundifolia

FAMILY
Bellflower (Campanulaceae)

NICKNAMES
bellflower, harebell, Scotch bluebell

BLOOM SEASON
May–September

HABITAT
open and rocky areas, from low to high elevations

HEIGHT
4–20″

SUN TOLERANCE
full sun, part shade

POLLINATORS
bees, self-pollination

Meet Bluebell: Bluebell served many purposes for Indigenous people in the Pacific Northwest. The Cree chewed roots to treat heart and lung diseases. Other tribes used it to make medicine or for protection. The Navajo people rubbed the flowers on their bodies to ward off witches, and hunters carried flowers to keep them safe. The Haida people believed picking bluebells brought rain, so they called them *blue rain flowers*. Bluebells also make a beautiful blue dye. Never eat any part of a wild plant unless you're 100 percent certain of its identification and how to consume it safely.

ORIGIN OF NAME

One look at this blue, bell-shaped flower, and you can quickly see how it got its common name. The scientific name is also suitable because *Campanula* means "little bell" and *rotundifolia* means "round leaves."

BIGGER ISN'T ALWAYS BETTER

This flower's nodding shape prevents large bees from accessing the pollen. So, the small to medium bees succeed in the obstacle course for bluebell pollen.

WITCHES' BREW

This flower is also commonly known as harebell, a name based on old folklore that witches drank the juices squeezed from this flower to transform themselves into hares (wild rabbits).

WILD ABOUT POETRY

This wildflower inspired poet Emily Dickinson's poem "Did the Harebell Lose Her Girdle?"

Upland Larkspur

Delphinium nuttallianum

WARNING!
All parts of this plant are toxic to humans and animals—do not eat.

FAMILY
Buttercup (Ranunculaceae)

NICKNAMES
thin-petal larkspur

BLOOM SEASON
March–August

HABITAT
dry, gravelly ground, from low to high elevations

HEIGHT
6–18"

SUN TOLERANCE
full sun

POLLINATORS
bees, butterflies, flies, hummingbirds

Meet Upland Larkspur: A little wildflower with a big warning—all parts of this plant are toxic. The younger the plant, the more toxic it is, and eating it can be fatal to humans and animals. Less severe symptoms include burning of the lips and mouth, difficulty breathing, muscle weakness and spasms, and a weak pulse. Indigenous Americans discovered a way to turn the poison into medicine that killed parasites. The violet-blue petals were used as decorations for special ceremonies and to make inks and dyes, which they used to paint their arrows and dye clothing and baskets.

ORIGIN OF NAME

Larkspur refers to the long petal resembling the back claw of a Meadowlark bird. In his famous writings, William Shakespeare called it lark's heel.

HOST A HUMMINGBIRD

If you want to attract hummingbirds to your yard, these beautiful violet-blue flowers are one of their favorites.

NATURAL SYMMETRY

This flower is symmetrical, meaning if divided down the middle, its two halves would look the same. Its balanced appearance is pleasing to the eye and a great example of natural symmetry.

OCCASIONALLY WHITE

These flowers typically bloom light blue to dark purple, but occasionally, you may spot a white blossom.

Explorer's Gentian

Gentiana calycosa

FAMILY
Gentian (Gentianaceae)

NICKNAMES
mountain bog gentian

BLOOM SEASON
July–October

HABITAT
Meadows, from low to high elevations

HEIGHT
8–20″

SUN TOLERANCE
full sun, part shade

POLLINATORS
bees

Meet Explorer's Gentian: The vibrant purple-blue flowers grow in clusters of up to three blooms. Each funnel-shaped cup opens into five petals speckled with yellow and dark blue spots and pointed tips. Look closely—a triangle-shaped part of the flower between the petals will help confirm your identification. There are 360 species in the genus *Gentiana*, each with different uses but one thing in common—they have inspired the paint industry. Gentian blue is a popular luxury car color that combines marine blue, cornflower blue, and Old Glory blue to mimic the purple-blue color of gentian wildflowers.

ORIGIN OF NAME

Gentiana is named after King Gentius, who ruled from 180 to 168 BCE and was considered the first person to use this plant for medicine.

PORSCHE PAINT

Porsche, a German company making luxury cars, offers Gentian Blue Metallic as a popular paint color choice.

STEMMING CLUES

To correctly identify this wildflower, look for a red stem with seven to nine pairs of opposite-growing leaves climbing it.

FAREWELL TO SUMMER

Explorer's gentian is one of the last wildflowers to bloom in fall, a grand finale signaling the end of the wildflower season.

Broadleaf Lupine

Lupinus latifolius

WARNING! This plant is poisonous to most animals if eaten raw—do not eat.

FAMILY
Pea (Fabaceae)

NICKNAMES
blue pea, old maid's bonnet, sundial, wild pea

BLOOM SEASON
June–August

HABITAT
moist open to shady woods and meadows, from middle to high elevations

HEIGHT
24–48"

SUN TOLERANCE
full sun, part shade

POLLINATORS
bees, beetles, bumblebees, butterflies, flies, honeybees, hummingbirds, wasps

Meet Lupine: Although ALL wildflowers are designed for pollination, lupine wins the award for most functional design. Hidden inside each lupine is a canoe-shaped spike (keel) that protects the flower's stamens (male parts) and pistils (female parts). When a pollinator lands on the lower petals, its weight pushes down on the petals, forcing the pollen-covered keel to lift, like a seesaw, and present itself to hungry pollinators who, unknowingly, rub against it as they feast on the pollen. Once a pollinator leaves, the keel retracts to its hiding place inside the petals.

ORIGIN OF NAME

Lupinus, Latin for "wolf," was so named because botanists once believed lupines greedily wolfed up nutrients, leaving the soil unhealthy for other plants. The opposite is actually true: Lupines fertilize soil, making it more nutritious for nearby plants.

LIVING SUNDIAL

Lupine is sometimes called sundial because its leaves act as a sundial, following the sun's path in the sky daily. At night, they fold up to protect themselves from the cold night air.

DELICIOUS AND CEREMONIAL

Indigenous Americans ate lupine in various ways, including making a relish to serve with manzanita cider. Lupine leaves were often burned as incense, and spiritual leaders believed chewing on them before ceremonial face-painting strengthened their powers.

STEMMING EXTINCTION

Lupines are the only known food source for the nearly extinct Karner blue butterfly. In mid-April, Karner blue larvae crawl up the wild lupine stems to feast on delicious new leaves.

Leafybract Aster

Symphyotrichum foliaceum

FAMILY
Composite/Aster (Asteraceae)

NICKNAMES
alpine leafybract aster, leafy aster

BLOOM SEASON
July–September

HABITAT
ditches, disturbed areas, moist but well-drained meadows, and springs, from low to high elevations

HEIGHT	SUN TOLERANCE	POLLINATORS
12–48″	full sun	bees, butterflies, and flies

Meet Leafybract Aster: These cheerful purple blooms are hot spots for pollinators, especially butterflies and native bees. In an Oregon State University study, students watched these flowers for several minutes and recorded every pollinator that visited. Sometimes, there were so many it was challenging to keep track. Asters attract native bees, which are important for our environment. Native bees help pollinate many plants we rely on for food, like fruits, vegetables, and nuts. But one out of every four native bee species is at risk of disappearing forever. Planting these wildflowers can help native bees.

Bees see in ultraviolet light, which makes the leafybract aster easy for it to spot.

ORIGIN OF NAME

The Greek word *aster* means "star" and refers to the star-like shape of this flower's head.

BLOOMING LOVE

In Greek mythology, people placed asters on the altars of the gods as symbols of love.

ASTERS AROUND THE GLOBE

There are more than 32,000 species of asters worldwide, found on every continent except Antarctica.

SYMPTOMS AND EVIL SPIRITS

Indigenous Americans used aster flowers to treat common colds, migraines, muscle spasms, and back pain. They also burned the flowers, hoping the smoke would protect them against evil spirits.

BROWN

Morning light shines through a pair of chocolate lilies in the Columbia River Gorge.

Chocolate Lily

Fritillaria affinis

FAMILY
Lily (Liliaceae)

NICKNAMES
checker lily, rice-root lily

BLOOM SEASON
April–June

HABITAT
grassy bluffs and prairies to coniferous forests and woodlands, from low to high elevations

HEIGHT
12–36"

SUN TOLERANCE
full sun, part shade

POLLINATORS
bees, flies, wasps

Meet Chocolate Lily: Many Indigenous Pacific Northwest tribes relied on this plant for food, with some calling it rice-root because its tiny, secondary bulbs (bulblets) resemble small grains of rice. Commonly, the bulbs were steamed; some also steamed the bitter-tasting seedpods. Roots and stems were also used for food, typically roasted. While they were once a common food source, harvesting chocolate lily bulbs today is highly discouraged because their population has decreased to a concerningly smaller size. Never eat any part of a wild plant unless you're 100 percent certain of its identification and how to consume it safely.

ORIGIN OF NAME

Fritillaria is a Latin word meaning "checkered dice box" that refers to the flower's checker-printed petals. *Affinis* means "related to," and represents all species in the entire genus.

BEES AND POLLEN

Several types of bees collect this flower's nectar and pollen, and sweat bees roll pollen balls for their larvae to grow inside.

RODENT FOOD

Mice, squirrels, voles, and other rodents enjoy eating the flowers' underground bulbs.

A PRACTICE IN PATIENCE

Chocolate lilies do not produce flowers yearly. Instead, they grow a wide "nurse leaf," which is excellent for absorbing sunlight. This leaf makes and stores food in the bulb for future blooms.

Piggyback

Tolmiea menziesii

FAMILY
Saxifrage (Saxifragaceae)

NICKNAMES
thousand mothers, youth-on-age

BLOOM SEASON
May–August

HABITAT
moist woods and streambanks, from low to middle elevations

HEIGHT
12–30"

SUN TOLERANCE
full shade

POLLINATORS
bees

Meet Piggyback: The piggyback plant is pollinated by bees but often grows deep in forests where bees rarely go. How do bees find them? Scientists discovered that, when seen through a bee's eyes, the pollen shines a bright, fluorescent red-orange color, making it easy to find. If you observe the pollen on the bee's legs, you'll see it's darker than the pollen on the flower. As the bees load the pollen behind their legs, they combine it with juicy nectar; as wet nectar mixes with dry pollen, the pollen's moisture content changes, giving it a darker red-orange shade.

ORIGIN OF NAME

This plant is known as the piggyback plant because the smaller "daughter" plants at the base of each stem resemble a parent giving their child a piggyback ride.

YOU GROW, GIRL

Piggyback plants reproduce with the help of their daughter plants. When these baby plants are ready, they detach from the stem, fall into the nearby soil, and take root, beginning the life cycle of new plants.

THE INSIDE SCOOP

Looking for the perfect roommate? Piggyback plants make great indoor houseplants.

LEAFING CLUES

You will know that you found the right plant if its leaves are wide and oblong and have short, sharp, jagged bristles covering the topside.

WILD-FLOWERS TO WATCH OUT FOR

Keep an eye out for these wildflowers and be sure to steer clear. Even though these flowers play an important role in our environment, they may have an unfortunate effect on humans—don't get too close.

Poison Oak

Toxicodendron diversilobum

FAMILY
Sumac (Anacardiaceas)

PETAL COLOR
white

BLOOM SEASON
May–June

HABITAT
forest openings, from low to high elevations

HEIGHT
12–96"

SUN TOLERANCE
full sun, part shade

POLLINATORS
bees

ORIGIN OF NAME

Toxicodendron is Latin for "poison tree," where *toxico* means "poison," and *dendron* means "tree." I think the name might be trying to tell us something.

SURPRISING BENEFITS

Birds eat the berries, and black-tail deer and moths eat the leaves. Honeybees and native bees gather nectar to make a bitter but non-toxic honey.

WARNING!
Poison oak contains an oil that may cause an itchy rash followed by bumps and blisters. Remember, *when you see leaves of three, let them be.*

Devil's-club

Oplopanax horridus

Devil's-club's sharp spines warn us not to get too close.

WARNING! This plant is covered in spines, which irritate your skin when touched.

FAMILY
Ginseng (Araliaceae)

PETAL COLOR
greenish white

BLOOM SEASON
May–July

HABITAT
moist woods and streambanks, at low elevations

HEIGHT
36–120"

SUN TOLERANCE
full sun, part shade

POLLINATORS
bees

ORIGIN OF NAME

Devil's-club's name comes from *hoplon*, meaning "weapon," and *panakos*, meaning "heal-all." This last fact may seem confusing, but it refers to other species in the ginseng family that are commonly used for medicine.

SURPRISING BENEFITS

Bears eat large quantities of devil's-club berries in midsummer and then spread the seeds in their droppings. Indigenous Americans burned this plant and used the charcoal for tattoo ink.

Stinging Nettle

Urtica dioica

FAMILY
Nettle (Urticaceae)

PETAL COLOR
white

FLOWER COLOR
reddish green

BLOOM SEASON
May–September

HABITAT
deep, rich soil near moisture, from low to high elevations

HEIGHT
36–108"

SUN TOLERANCE
part shade to full shade

POLLINATORS
wind

ORIGIN OF NAME

The genus name *Urtica* comes from the Latin word for "sting."

WARNING!
This plant is covered with tiny stinging hairs. If touched, the tips of the hairs break off easily, leaving very irritating chemicals in your skin that cause painful rashes and extreme discomfort.

SURPRISING BENEFITS

Stinging nettle provides a place for many butterfly species to lay their eggs and shelters the adults in winter so they can lay eggs and restart the cycle. Indigenous Americans used nettles for food, tea, and medicine to treat arthritis.

POWER TO THE POLLINATORS

Pollinator: *An animal that helps carry pollen from the anther (male part) of a flower to the stigma (female part) of a flower so the plant can make a seed*

A wildflower's most important job is to reproduce, or make new plants. In order to make new plants, it must make seeds. However, making a seed is a complicated process. Pollen (the dusty powder that contains sperm) needs to be taken from the anther of a flower to the stigma of the same or another flower. This critical process is called pollination, and, once it's complete, the plant can make seeds for new plants to grow.

Don't forget that wildflowers are held in the ground with roots. This means they can't move. So, how do they get the precious pollen they need for survival from one plant to another without moving? Ninety percent of flowering plants need help from pollinators—insects and animals that can carry the pollen. Luckily, there are more than 200,000 varieties of pollinators in the world to help them, including bats, bees, beetles, birds, butterflies, flies, hummingbirds, and moths.

Birds like this Goldfinch
are pollinators too.

POLLINATION: How Pollinators Help Plants Make New Seeds

Insects and animals carry pollen from the male part of a flower (anther) to the female part (stigma) of a flower so the plant can make a new seed.

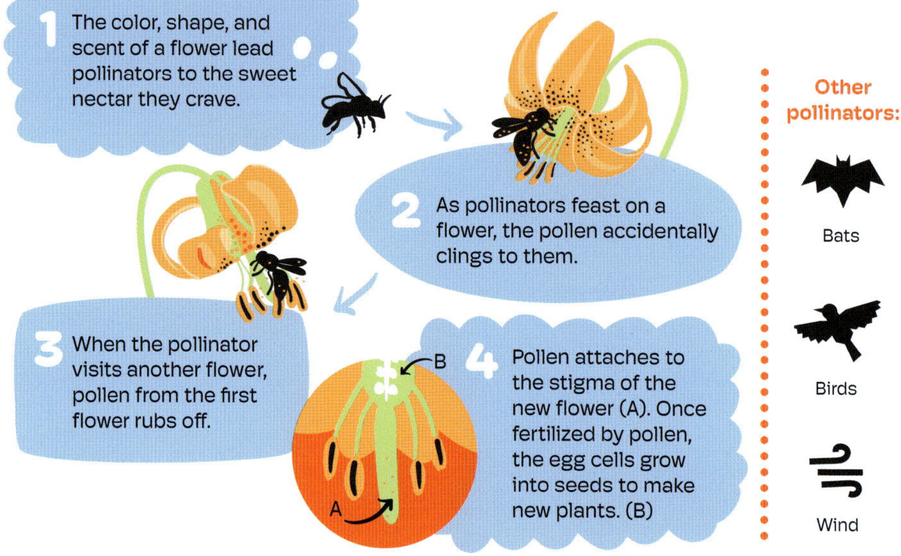

This diagram shows how pollinators help plants make seeds. Ninety percent of flowering plants need help from pollinators.

In the other 10 percent of flowering plants, some can pollinate themselves (self-pollinate), and some are pollinated by wind or water.

Pollinators Help People

Imagine your favorite food. Is it a fruit? Vegetable? Is it made from corn or wheat? Or sweetened with sugar or honey? Chances are a pollinator helped make it possible. One out of every three bites of food you eat comes from the hard work of pollinators.

Pollinators also pollinate plants that humans use to make clothing fabrics, like cotton and hemp. They pollinate plants and trees we use to make plastics, building supplies, and more. How would your life be different without pollinators?

Pollinators Need Your Help

Pollinators are beneficial for our survival, but they also need our help to survive. Threats due to climate change, disease, misuse of chemicals, and pollution make it harder for pollinators to

survive each year. For those of you who enjoy seeing wildflowers, chasing butterflies, eating chocolate, and licking honey off a spoon, here are some ways you can help pollinators survive.

- Plant a garden with native flowering plants and provide shallow water sources with something pollinators can perch on while they sip.
- Turn off outside lights at night. Moths and nocturnal insects are attracted to the artificial light source but can die from touching it.
- Hanging bat houses and birdhouses will encourage these pollinators to come to your yard.
- Pesticides can harm pollinators, so buy fruits, vegetables, and honey grown by local farmers who don't use pesticides on their crops.
- Thank a pollinator today.

Pollinators Have Preferences

If you spend time in a garden or field of wildflowers, you will notice which flowers usually swarm with bees and which are visited by butterflies. You likely have preferences about what foods you eat, and pollinators have favorites too. They choose the plants they prefer based on the flowers' color, shape, and scent. The relationship between pollinators and their preferred flowers is defined by a group of characteristics known as pollinator syndrome.

MEET THE POLLINATORS

Bats

FLOWER PREFERENCES

COLOR
dull white; sometimes green or purple

SMELL
strong, musty, fruity

SHAPE
bowl-shaped flowers

PREFERRED WILDFLOWERS
evening primrose, night-blooming phlox

Bats are skilled nocturnal pollinators, meaning they're most active at night. They play a vital role in pollinating more than 530 plants—mostly fruits. Bats are fantastic seed spreaders, flying long distances with fruit and pollen in their clutches. They eat the tasty part of the fruit and discard the rest, spreading seeds and pollen wherever they go. It's a win-win for bats and the plants they help grow. Need help controlling mosquitoes? Bats are especially good at hunting insects. Invite these helpful mammals into your yard by hanging bat boxes.

DID YOU KNOW?
Bats pollinate more than 300 kinds of fruit, especially those that grow in the tropics.

Bees

Being hairy comes in handy when gathering sticky pollen.

FLOWER PREFERENCES

COLOR
blue, ultraviolet, white, and yellow

SMELL
fresh, mild, sweet

SHAPE
shallow flowers with a broad tube and landing platform they can perch upon

PREFERRED WILDFLOWERS
grass widow, northwest balsamroot, upland larkspur, yellow monkey-flower

Bees are hairy, making it easy for pollen to stick to them. There are 75 species of bees in the Pacific Northwest, including bumblebees, carpenter bees, honeybees, mason bees, and sweat bees. Bees are the only insect species capable of getting all their dietary needs from flowers. Bees are attracted to many colors of wildflowers, but you won't see them on red flowers. This is because they see ultraviolet, so they cannot see red.

DID YOU KNOW?
Bees are also the only insects that make food that humans can eat. You guessed it—honey! Globally, about 100 million hives produce 1.8 million metric tons of honey every year.

Bees see ultraviolet light. This is how you would see a sunflower if you were a bee.

Beetles

In addition to being pollinators, ladybugs are also good for eating unwanted pests in your garden.

FLOWER PREFERENCES

COLOR
green, white

SMELL
fruity or stinky

SHAPE
bowl-shaped, flat

PREFERRED WILDFLOWERS
beargrass, false Solomon's seal, Oregon sunshine

Bees get all the buzz because they make honey, but the most common pollinators are beetles. With more than 350,000 species, beetles are the largest insect order in the world. Beetles are messy eaters—sloppily munching flowers and leaves, scattering seeds and pollen all around them. After a meal, they deposit seed- and pollen-filled droppings wherever they go, spreading seeds even farther. Beetles also eat wood, leaves, roots, fungi, other insects, animal remains, debris, nectar, and pollen. Gardeners love beetles, like ladybugs, because they eat unwanted pests. Beetles are also expert decomposers, helping break down dead plant and animal matter.

DID YOU KNOW?
Beetles are known to use the flowers they pollinate as their toilet, earning them the nickname of "mess and soil" pollinators.

Butterflies

This Swallowtail butterfly is attracted to this red columbine for its color and how well its curled mouthpart can reach into the flower's narrow tubes.

FLOWER PREFERENCES

COLOR
brightly colored flowers, such as purple and red

SMELL
faint but fresh

SHAPE
narrow tube flowers with a wide landing pad on which to perch

PREFERRED WILDFLOWERS
California poppy, penstemon, western buttercup

Butterflies are incredible long-distance flyers! Each year, butterflies fly thousands of miles along nectar corridors, popular routes with well-known flowers they can rely on for food. Equipped with a hollow, coiled-up mouth-part called a proboscis, butterflies use it like a straw to drink nectar and nutrients from flowers. When you spot butterflies on the beach, watch them closely. You might catch them with their proboscis in the sand, slurping up essential nutrients.

DID YOU KNOW?
Butterflies lack a strong sense of smell but have great vision. Unlike bees, butterflies *can* see red.

These Swallowtail butterflies are using their sucking mouthparts to drink nutrients from wet soil.

Flies

FLOWER PREFERENCES

COLOR
pale to dark brown or purple

SMELL
very strong and stinky

SHAPE
shallow flowers shaped like a funnel or trap

PREFERRED WILDFLOWERS
false Solomon's seal, miner's lettuce

Flies eat decaying matter and enjoy stinky treats such as rotting fruit, meat, vegetables, animal and plant secretions, and even human feces. Some plants, such as skunk cabbage, give off the scent of rotting meat to attract flies for pollination. Flies are often considered annoying pests, but if you like chocolate, you may want to reconsider your opinion about them because flies are the primary pollinators for cacao trees, which produce chocolate!

DID YOU KNOW?
Some flies, such as hoverflies, have black and yellow stripes that make them look like bees. How can you tell the difference? Flies have one set of wings, whereas bees have two.

Hummingbirds

Hummingbirds have long, slender bills and straw-like tongues to sip nectar.

FLOWER PREFERENCES

COLOR
bright orange, red, and yellow

SMELL
very mild smell or none

SHAPE
tube-shaped flowers

PREFERRED WILDFLOWERS
columbine, lupine, penstemon

More than 2,000 different species of birds are pollinators, but hummingbirds are the most famous. Flapping their tiny wings up to 90 beats per second burns many calories, so hummingbirds must eat a lot! They need to eat enough food to equal half their body weight daily, leading them to feed every 10 to 15 minutes and visit 1,000 to 2,000 flowers daily! In addition to drinking nectar, they eat spiders, insect larvae, and small insects for protein. If you were a hummingbird, how many pounds of food would you need to eat every day?

DID YOU KNOW?

Hummingbirds have long, slender bills and straw-like tongues that are great for drinking nectar. They can perch on a flower while they sip, but they don't need to because they can also hover.

Moths

FLOWER PREFERENCES

COLOR
white or pale shades of pink, purple, and red

SMELL
strong, sweet-smelling scents released at night

SHAPE
regular or tube-shaped flowers without a lip

PREFERRED WILDFLOWERS
prairie star, trillium, white bog orchid

Silk fabric is made possible by moths. Silk moth caterpillars use fine threads to make cocoons in which they transform from a caterpillar into a moth. Since ancient times, humans have collected these cocoons and used the threads to make silk fabric. Want more moths to visit your garden? The first thing to do is limit porch and garden lights at night. Moths navigate by the light of the moon and the stars. Therefore, artificial light (like the light from a lightbulb) confuses them and can prove deadly. Planting light-colored, night-blooming flowers like evening primrose will also attract moths.

DID YOU KNOW?
Moths and butterflies look alike. Notice: Moths have thick bodies, short, feathery antennae, and their wings rest open along their body. Butterflies have thin bodies, long, straight, or clubbed antennae, and their wings rest closed and upright.

LEAVE NO TRACE: *LEAVE SOME FOR THE BEES, PLEASE*

Only if we understand will we care. Only if we care will we help. Only if we help shall we all be saved.
—Jane Goodall

Caring for nature means taking care of nature. No one likes to hike to a beautiful place to find dirty toilet paper in the bushes. As nature enthusiasts who love exploring the wild, we know how special these places are. We are responsible for keeping them this way.

We can follow a simple practice to ensure that our adventures today do not compromise our adventures tomorrow. We call this practice *Leave No Trace*, which means learning how to be in nature without leaving any clues that you were ever there. In other words, everything you bring along must return home with you. Every food wrapper. Every bottle cap. Every orange peel and pistachio shell.

Orange peels count as trash and take about six months to fully decompose.

No matter how many times you have been somewhere, it's always worth the time to stop and enjoy the view.

How to Leave No Trace

1. **Know Before You Go.** The more prepared you are, the more fun you will have. Weather can change quickly, and who wants to run out of snacks? To be safe and have fun, always bring what you need, including maps, raincoats, food, and water.

2. **Travel on the Trail.** Walking on the trail will help keep your feet off the wildflowers.

3. **Pack It In, Pact It Out.** Pick up your trash because it's gross not to. It's also doubtful that someone else will pick it up for you. Who wants to pick up someone else's trash?

4. **Leave Some for the Bees, Please.** Wildflowers provide seeds, nectar, and pollen that animals, butterflies, insects, and small birds need to survive. Although the wildflowers are beautiful, picking even one causes damage to the environment.

5. **Respect and Protect.** In nature, we are visitors to wild animals and their homes. Always observe animals from a safe distance, and be careful where you walk, sit, and throw down your picnic blanket.

6. **Be Considerate of Others.** People visit natural areas for various activities, many of which are better appreciated in the quiet. Make sure your fun in nature does not disturb anyone else. Plus—the quieter you are, the more likely you are to see animals. Speaking of animals, dogs like to follow rules too. But, when it comes to packing a leash and reading the pet rules on a park sign, they need your help. They also need a hand—or, should I say, an opposable thumb—to carry out their poop bags.

Wildflowers "grow by the inch but die by the foot," so watch where you step.

MEET
Ashley Erdely

PHOTO BY KELLY TURSO

NICKNAMES
Mama

BIRTHPLACE
Traverse City, Michigan

CURRENT HABITAT
White Salmon, Washington

At the end of the day, your feet should be dirty, your hair messy, and your eyes sparkling.
—Shanti

Meet Ashley: Growing up in rural Northern Michigan on a 130-acre llama ranch, Ashley considered animals her best friends and nature her playground. Most of her family vacations were spent camping and visiting national parks. Later, as a teenager, she attended a life-changing National Outdoor Leadership School (NOLS) course. These early experiences in nature inspired her passion for connecting children with nature and pursuing education. In 2005, equipped with a teaching license and a contract for her first job, she journeyed westward along the 45th parallel to the Pacific Northwest. There, she established her home in the picturesque Columbia River Gorge, where she now lives with her husband, daughter, and dog, surrounded by more than 750 distinctive wildflower species.

ORIGIN OF NAME

As a young child, a family friend nicknamed her "Daisy," perhaps planting a seed for a flowery future to come.

INSPIRATIONS

Things in nature that inspire her include wings, sleeping under the stars, jellyfish, moving water, and the many colors in a single meadow.

ACKNOWLEDGMENTS

Thank you to every single person over the last five years who has asked me, "How's your book?" It humbled me every time just to know you remembered. Each one of you kept the dream alive and possible.

To Kirby—thank you for proving to me that if I stepped back and focused on creating my dream, I would be supported, and it would work. I said it sixteen years ago and I would say it again today, "Absolutely."

To Iyla Grace—thank you for your patience whenever I disappeared into "Book World." You're my hero, my inspiration, and my greatest teacher.

Thank you to my family, "framily," and incredible friends. I'm speechless and grateful to you all.

Wendy Martin—thank you for believing in me and teaching me how to look in the mirror to see for myself. You're still my hero today.

To Brandon Sprouse—working with you on early proposal designs was one of the most special experiences I have ever had. Thank you for bringing my ideas to life in your thoughtful and beautiful designs.

To the hundreds of kids, parents, and educators who were a part of the research, development, testing, and creation of this book—thank you. Special thanks to Aneka Diem for your thoughtful edits and Becky Williams and your awesome fourth graders who helped me write the "Leave No Trace" chapter.

To botanists David Giblin and, especially, Krista K. Thie—I am so grateful for your willingness to share your knowledge, time, and energy with me for this project. I learned so much from you and am deeply appreciative.

To the extremely talented Nancy Harbert, Peter Marbach, Linda Steider, and Kelly Turso, whose photography brings this book to life.

To my agent, Jenny Stephens at Sterling Lord Literistic, thank you for all your enthusiasm, guidance, and support. Cheers to your young naturalist and all the wildflowers you'll explore together.

To Ryan Harrington at Timber Press—when I sent my proposal out into the world, I knew it would find a match, but I never could have imagined such a "kismet" experience. It's been a pleasure to work with you, and thank you for making me feel valued and included in this process.

To Sarah Milhollin, Cobi Lawson, and all the great folks at Timber Press. Being new to this field, I feel incredibly grateful to have had you as my guides through this journey. I knew I was in good hands, every step of the way.

To the incredibly talented folks at Bologna Sandwich—working with you brought my ideas to life and goosebumps to my skin.

Thank you to the many people who generously shared their professional expertise with me along this journey, especially Margot Angstrom, Andrea Bemis, Jeanette Burkhardt, Mary Cassells, Eileen Garvin, Kevin and Laura Haspela, Joan Jerman, Stacy Karacostas, Joanna Kaufman, Lisa Kosglow, Ted Lee, Matthew Lore, Janet O'Sullivan, Andrew Parks, Jennifer Rowlen, and Mark Turner.

To Claire Gilchrist—thank you for sharing your authorly experience, sincere and insightful edits, and for be-*leaf*-ing in me.

To Lindsey Hales—thank you for your tremendous editing support and for doing so with genuine care and absolute integrity. Sharing the final drafts with you made this project come alive and I truly don't know where I would be without you.

To the incredible librarians of the White Salmon Library and all the local bookshops, especially Waucoma Books, who keep the magic of printed books and small-town community alive.

Thank you to all the children I have ever had the privilege of sharing time in nature with. Magical moments in nature with you remind adults how vital the connection to our natural environment truly is.

And, dear reader, thank you for being a part of this journey to reconnect with nature, each other, and ourselves.

GLOSSARY

Abiotic Nonliving things in nature such as rocks, sun, and water

Abiotic pollinators Nonliving pollinators such as water and wind

Achene A fruit holding the plant's seed

Adapt To grow and change in response to environmental changes

Adaptation Changes in features or behaviors that allow for survival in an altered environment

Annual Meaning "every year," referring to a plant that needs to be planted from seed each year

Anther Male reproductive part; the plant part of the stamen that makes and stores pollen

Apomixis A plant able to reproduce independently without fertilization

Bald A high-elevation clearing on a mountain summit, crest, or outcrop covered in dense native grasses and shrubs in areas where heavy forest growth would be expected

Botanical name A unique name given to each plant by botanists, who study plants

Botanist A person who studies plants

Botany The scientific study of plants

Bract A small leaf or leaflike structure at the base of a flower or flower cluster

Bulb Underground bud with thickened fleshy scales, as in an onion (*see* corm)

Bulblet A small or secondary bulb

Calyx The flower's structure, made of sepals, that typically encloses the corolla

Carnivore An animal that eats meat

Common name Nonscientific name of a species, which often varies regionally

Composite flower A flower made up of hundreds of tiny flowers that, together, look like one larger flower

Corm Underground bud with thickened fleshy scales, as in an onion (*see* bulb)

Corolla The flower's structure formed by petals, which often contains nectar at its base

Cross-pollination Pollination of one flower with pollen of another, different, flower

Cultural keystone species Plant or animal that is especially significant to a culture or group of people

Decompose To break down dead or decomposing plant or animal materials and recycle essential nutrients to return to the soil

Decomposer An organism that feeds on and breaks down dead plants and animals

Disk flower One of the tiny tubular flowers covering the disk-shaped head of a composite flower

Diurnal A species that is active in daytime

Drought-resistant Plants that are naturally adapted to survive dry growing conditions

Echolocation A process by which nocturnal animals find their way in the dark by producing sound waves that are reflected off an object

Ecosystem All the living (animals, microorganisms, plants) and nonliving (rocks, sun, water) parts of an environment

Edible Able to be eaten

Elevation How high you are above sea level

Endangered species A species of plant or animal in danger of becoming extinct

Endemic A plant that is native to a place and found only in that particular area

Environment The living and nonliving things with which an organism interacts

Extinction The state of a species of plant or animal that has disappeared permanently

Family A scientific grouping of similar genus groups

Fauna Animals of a particular habitat or region

Fertilization The process after pollination when the male and female reproductive parts of a plant join to produce seeds

Filament The slender support holding the anther upright

Fire-resistant Does not burn easily

Flora Plants of a particular habitat or region

Floret A small flower, or one of the small flowers, that makes up the head of a composite flower

Foliage Leaves

Genus A group of organisms closely related because they share one or more common characteristic

Geophyte A plant that stores energy and water in its special underground organs (bulbs, corms, rhizomes, and so on)

Germinate To begin to grow

Habitat Place where a plant or animal lives

Heliotropic Growing or turning toward the light

Herbivore An animal that eats only plants

Host plant A plant that another species (plant or animal) lives on for survival

Indigenous Occurring naturally in a particular region or environment (*see* native)

Inflorescence A group, or cluster, of flowers arranged together on a stem

Invasive Describes a species that is not native to an area and causes economic or environmental harm

Keel Two connected petals that hold the pistil and stamens, typically found on the flower of a papilionaceous (pea, bean, or grain) plant

Larva A young wingless insect form (often wormlike) that hatches from insect eggs, such as a grub or caterpillar

Lobe Curved or pointed parts that stick out from the main part of a flower

Metamorphosis The process of a larva transforming into an adult, which involves a series of changes in the animal's body

Microclimate The climate of a small, restricted area that differs from its surrounding climate

Migration Animals moving from one place to another during certain times of the year

Mutualism A relationship between two species where both species benefit or help each other

Native Occurring naturally in a particular region or environment (*see* indigenous)

Naturalist A person who studies the natural world

Nectar Sugary fluid made by flowers to attract animal and insect pollinators

Nectary Flower pouch that stores nectar

Nocturnal A species that is active at night, such as bats and moths

Ovary A flower's female reproductive part; the base of the pistil, containing one or more eggs (ovules)

Ovules Small, egg-like female reproductive parts of the flower that become seeds after being fertilized

Perennial Means "recurring;" a plant that does not need to be replanted from seed each year

Petal An individual segment of the corolla that surrounds the flower's reproductive structures, typically colorful

Petiole A slender stem that supports the blade of a leaf

Photosynthesis The process by which green plants use energy from the sun to make food

Pistil A flower's female reproductive part; the part of a plant where pollen is delivered and seeds are made, comprising the stigma, style, and ovary

Pollen Microscopic powdery substance (usually yellow) containing the sperm that a flower needs to grow a new plant, also considered a male reproductive part

Pollinated Fertilized state of a flower after its female parts have received pollen from the male parts of the same (or a different) flower

Pollination Process of spreading pollen from the male part of a flower to the female parts of the same species of flower, resulting in seeds and fruits

Pollinator An insect or animal that helps carry pollen from the male part of a flower (anther) to the female part of a flower (stigma) so the plant can make a seed

Pollinator syndrome A group of characteristics (color, shape, scent) that define the relationship between pollinators and their preferred flowers

Proboscis The long, coiled, sucking mouth part of invertebrates, such as bees, butterflies, and moths

Ray flower A small flower or floret resembling a petal that surrounds the disk-shaped heads of composite plants, such as a sunflower

Reproduce To make new offspring (new plants)

Scientific name The unique name given to a species (plant or animal) by scientists

Seed The part of the plant capable of growing and producing a new plant

Seed capsule The part of a fruit that holds the seeds

Self-pollination Process by which a plant fertilizes itself without the help of a pollinator

Sepal Part of the outer part of a flower that surrounds and supports the petals; usually small and green but can be colorful and mistaken for a petal

Species A group of plants or animals with similar characteristics that can reproduce

Stalk The stem of a plant supporting a flower, fruit, or leaf

Stamen A flower's male reproductive part; the feathery part of the flower that makes pollen

Stem The main support of the plant parts, usually above ground; the main stalk

Steppe (pronounced *step*) Land that is dry, usually flat, and covered with grass

Stigma A flower's female reproductive part; the sticky top of the pistil where pollen lands during pollination

Style Female reproductive part; the tube-like stalk that connects the stigma to the ovary

Symbiotic relationship Relationship between two or more species in which both benefit

Symmetrical Describing an object that looks the same on all sides

Taxonomic system A way of organizing living things into groups based on common characteristics

Taxonomy The science of naming, describing, and classifying organisms

Tepal An outer part of a flower not easily identified as a petal or sepal

Threatened species Plant or animal group likely to become endangered without protection and management

Toxic Containing a poison or toxin

Trichomes Little hairs on leaves that help the plant conserve water by reflecting heat and reducing how much dry air can blow across its surface

Umbel An inflorescence, or cluster, of tiny flowers that radiate outward from the tip of the main stem, resembling an umbrella

Weed A naturally occurring, seed-producing flower that grows without the help of humans in a place where it's not wanted

Wildflower A naturally occurring, seed-producing flower that grows without the help of humans

PHOTOGRAPHY CREDITS

Illustrations by Bologna Sandwich

Glacier NPS, 171 (top)
Jeff Bleam, 107 (bottom)
KEVIN ELSBY/Alamy.com, 163
Laura Gaudette, licensed under the Creative Commons Attribution 4.0 International license, 169
Linda Steider, 11, 24, 27, 29, 33, 38, 39, 44, 45, 50, 51 (top), 52, 53, 56, 57, 58, 59, 62, 64, 68, 69, 70, 71, 73, 74, 75, 76, 80, 81, 82, 85 (bottom), 86, 87, 90, 91, 92, 93, 101, 102, 103, 106, 107 (top), 108, 109, 110, 112, 113, 114, 115 (bottom), 118, 119, 123, 125 (top), 128, 129, 131, 137, 138, 140, 141, 142, 143, 144, 145, 146, 147 (bottom), 148, 150, 159, 161, 164, 165, 166, 167, 168, 171 (bottom), 173
Nancy Harbert, 35, 54, 55, 60, 61, 66, 67, 77, 78, 98, 99, 104, 105, 115 (top), 116, 117, 122, 136, 147 (top), 151, 155, 156,
Peter Marbach, 23, 94, 126
USFWS/Tom Koerner, 130

Flickr

CC BY-SA 2.0

Andreas Rockstein, 46, 47, 62
Matt Lavin, 85 (top), 97, 111, 120, 121, 124
Peter Abrahamsen, 153 (top)
Randi Hausken, 25
Willamette Biology, 84

CC BY 2.0

Andrey Zharkikh, 42, 48, 51 (bottom), 72, 96, 125 (bottom), 132, 133, 134, 135
CC BY-ND 2.0
Ed Ogle, 49
Jan-Erik Finnberg, 100
John Tann, 157
Liz West, 79
Marilyn Peddle, 139
Peter Stevens, 83, 152, 153 (bottom)
tdlucas5000, 88

INDEX

C

D

M

N

O

P

T

U

V

W